W9-CQZ-261

PETERSON'S

SAT*

MATH
FLASH

The Quick Way to Build Math Power for the SAT—and Beyond

Michael R. Crystal

*SAT IS A REGISTERED TRADEMARK OF THE COLLEGE ENTRANCE EXAMINATION BOARD, WHICH WAS NOT INVOLVED IN THE PRODUCTION OF, AND DOES NOT ENDORSE, THIS PRODUCT.

Peterson's
Princeton, New Jersey

Printed in the United States of America

10 9 8 7 6 5 4 3 2 1

ACKNOWLEDGMENTS

Every problem in this book, as well as being modeled after the SAT, reflects some person or situation I've encountered while composing *SAT Math Flash*. I greatly appreciate all of these friends who have provided inspiration and kept the process of coming up with new problems fun.

Joan Carris, author of *SAT Word Flash*, although mentioned in only one problem, has kindly let me draw on previous work we've done together in *SAT Success* and *Panic Plan for the SAT*. I am honored to be able to say that we have and continue to work well together.

I am grateful to BBN, Inc., of Cambridge, MA, for providing me with the facilities, environment, and occasional office supplies to create this book.

Michael R. Crystal
December 1996

CONTENTS

ABOUT SAT MATH FLASH

SAT Math Flash is your private tutor. Instead of trying to cram more arithmetic, algebra, and geometry lessons onto thinner paper, with smaller type, *SAT Math Flash* recreates two math SATs and walks you through them. If you have difficulty with a question, you can read the detailed answer that follows on the next page. When you understand a problem, you can check the answer quickly and instead focus on areas where you need to study.

To write *SAT Math Flash* we analyzed ETS-provided preprints of two SATs. For each problem on the SAT, we wrote a new problem that tests the same skills at the same difficulty level and placed it in our test in the same position as we found it on the SAT. This guarantees that what you're working with here models what you'll see when you sit down to take the "real thing." The structure is the same; the skills tested are the same; the difficulty of the problems is the same; and the types of problems are the same.

We then wrote detailed answers to each of the 120 problems, describing explicitly the math skill that each question tests. On page 141 we provide a *Concept-to-Problem* index. If after reviewing a problem solution you decide that you need more practice with a particular math skill, you can individualize your study plan and save time by looking the skill up in the index and focusing on those problems that exercise the skill.

HOW TO USE *SAT MATH FLASH*

Dig right in! The best practice for the SAT is to do SAT problems. As you're doing each problem:

1. *Try to spot what skill is being tested.* For example, when you're asked to solve for x in the equation: $1 + 2 + 3 + 4 + 5 + 6 = 3 + 7 + x$; notice that by grouping the 1 with the 2, and the 3 with the 4, on the left side of the equation it becomes clear that x is just $5 + 6$. This isn't just an exercise in math skills. When you can see what

skill a problem tests, you'll be able to answer the question faster and more accurately.

2. *Do the problem completely.* Too often, someone studying for the test will skip a problem, thinking, "I can do that," only to find out during the actual SAT that the problem wasn't as simple as it looked. If you find a problem in this book easy, do it quickly, fill in the answer, and just look to see if you got it right. Then go on to the next problem.

3. *If you get a problem wrong, stop.* Use the discussion to figure out what you didn't know but needed to. If it's a theorem or a definition, memorize it. Remember, these problems come from the SAT; you will see the same skill tested again.

4. *Also, when you get a problem wrong circle the problem number in the Concept-to-Problem index, on page 141.* Having done this, when you're through with each exam you can look and see what topic areas you're having the most trouble with and focus your attention on those.

When you're done with each test, you should:

1. *Be comfortable with the SAT format.* This is important. When test day comes around you don't want to have to learn the peculiarities of "gridding-in" an answer. If you'd like more practice with real SATs, buy the book *10 SATs* published by ETS. It's a compilation of ten old tests.

2. *Have gained insight into what your individual strengths and weaknesses are.* If you diligently marked the problems you got wrong in the *Concept-to-Problem* index, you will be able to read off the number of problems you answered incorrectly for each problem category.

3. *Identify those skills that you're having difficulty with and:*
   - Use the *Concept-to-Problem* index to find and rework the problems that test the skill
   - Review your math textbook

- Work through an SAT "test prep" book, such as *SAT Success* or *Panic Plan for the SAT*; or,
- Ask your teacher for additional practice problems.

Whatever method you choose to learn the material, having gone through *Math Flash* enables you to focus on just those areas that need work.

4. *Keep Practicing*. The more problems you do, the more familiar you'll be with the SAT and the skills it tests. No question, this familiarity will get you a higher score.

Despite changes to the SAT over the years, its purpose and method are still basically the same as always:

1. The SAT math section tests your Arithmetic, Algebra I, and Geometry skills.

2. There are 60 (50 on the PSAT) questions consisting of 35 five-choice questions (25 on the PSAT), 15 quantitative comparison questions, and 10 grid-ins.

3. You have roughly one minute per problem.

4. You start with a score of 200 for writing your name, get approximately ten points for each correct answer, and lose approximately 2.5 points for each incorrect answer. The best possible score is 800.

Good luck. The first test begins on page 5.

TEST I

SECTION 1

This section consists of 25 problems and five possible answer choices for each. For each problem, select the answer choice that represents the best solution and shade the corresponding oval.

---

1. A half hour can be divided into 30 1-minute periods or 1 30-minute period. Into how many other same size periods can you divide a half hour if each period must be an integer number of minutes?

   (A) 2
   (B) 3
   (C) 4
   (D) 5
   (E) 6

Note: Figure not drawn to scale.
$x < 90°$

2. Which of the following best describes a?

   (A) $3 < a < 4$
   (B) $a = 1$
   (C) $a = 5$
   (D) $1 < a < 5$
   (E) $1 < a < 7$

---

1. Ⓐ Ⓑ Ⓒ Ⓓ Ⓔ

2. Ⓐ Ⓑ Ⓒ Ⓓ Ⓔ

Answer #1:   Ⓔ

Formula: • 30 = 2 × 3 × 5

Concept: • Factoring and prime factors

You are asked the different ways of dividing 30 into integer parts. Dividing something into even portions suggests a solution that uses prime factors. Assuming you haven't memorized the prime factors of 30, your first step is to compute them. Looking at 30, you should immediately recognize that it is divisible by 10: 30 = 3 × 10. Three is the first prime factor. 10 = 2 × 5, each of which are primes, so the prime factors of 30 are 2, 3, and 5.

Any divisor of 30 will be the product of the prime factors of 30, so you must now construct all of the products of the prime factors of 30. I like to do this in ascending order. First off, 2 and 3 are clearly factors, in fact they are prime factors: 2 × 15 = 3 × 10 = 30. Is 4? No, because there is no way of generating a 4 by multiplying 2, 3, and 5. The next factor is 5, a prime factor: 5 × 6 = 30.

You can stop checking after 5 and 6 because any number greater than 5 that can divide 30 must do so fewer than 6 times and we've checked all of the positive integers less than 6. So, 2, 3, and 5 are divisors of 30, as well as 15, 10, and 6 (the numbers by which 2, 3, and 5 have to be multiplied to generate 30). There are 6 ways of dividing 30 into integer portions.

Answer #2:   Ⓓ

Formulas: • In a triangle, the sum of the lengths of two sides is greater than the length of the third side.
• Pythagorean theorem: $a^2 + b^2 = c^2$

Concept: • Triangle geometry

Because the figure is not drawn to scale, you should feel free to re-draw the unconstrained aspects of the picture. Imagine the extreme case where x is very small. In this case you'd have a picture like A:

As x shrinks, a approaches the difference between the two other sides: $4 - 3 = 1$.

At the other extreme, imagine case B with the side of length 3 being stretched out almost, but not quite, perpendicular to the side of length 4—it can't be exactly perpendicular because you are told $x < 90°$.

By applying the Pythagorean theorem, as x approaches a right angle, a^2 approaches $3^2 + 4^2 = 5^2$. So a can get as large as, but not equal to, 5.

3. What mathematical expression describes the product of two numbers being divided by their difference?

   (A) $\dfrac{xy}{x-y}$

   (B) $\dfrac{x+y}{x-y}$

   (C) $\dfrac{x-y}{xy}$

   (D) $\dfrac{xy}{x+y}$

   (E) $\dfrac{x-y}{x+y}$

4. $\left(x - \dfrac{1}{x}\right)^2 + 4 =$

   (A)   4

   (B)   5

   (C) $x^2 - \left(\dfrac{1}{x}\right)^2 + 4$

   (D) $x^2 + \left(\dfrac{1}{x}\right)^2$

   (E) $\left(x + \dfrac{1}{x}\right)^2$

3.   (A)   (B)   (C)   (D)   (E)

4.   (A)   (B)   (C)   (D)   (E)

Anser #3:   Ⓐ

Concept: • Word problems

This problem tests your ability to create a mathematical expression from an English one. The method here is to work phase by phrase. From the problem,

You read:	*You write:*
1. The product of two numbers	xy
2. being divided by	$\dfrac{xy}{}$
3. their difference	$\dfrac{xy}{x-y}$

Answer #4:   Ⓔ

Formulas: • $\left(x + \dfrac{1}{x}\right)^2 = x^2 + 2 + \left(\dfrac{1}{x}\right)^2$

• $\left(x - \dfrac{1}{x}\right)^2 = x^2 - 2 + \left(\dfrac{1}{x}\right)^2$

• FOIL (First, Outer, Inner, Last)

Concept: • Polynomial arithmetic

The quantities $\left(x + \dfrac{1}{x}\right)^2$ and $\left(x - \dfrac{1}{x}\right)^2$ arise often in SAT problems because a) they look complicated with an x in the denominator of a fraction; and b) the middle term lacks an x.

To solve this problem, start with the $\left(x - \dfrac{1}{x}\right)^2$. Expand it out to get $x^2 - 2 + \left(\dfrac{1}{x}\right)^2$. Now, add 4 to the middle term to get $x^2 + 2 + \left(\dfrac{1}{x}\right)^2$. You should now be able to recognize this as $\left(x + \dfrac{1}{x}\right)^2$.

5. If the cost of a 4-minute telephone call is $0.24, then the cost of a 15-minute call at the same rate is:

(A) $0.60
(B) $0.65
(C) $0.75
(D) $0.90
(E) $1.11

6. At a carnival, a booth is set up with a game that costs 15¢ to play. The first person to play wins a penny, the second person a nickel, the third person a dime, and the fourth a quarter. The cycle is repeated with the fifth person winning a penny and so on. After 43 people have played the game how much money has the booth made, net profit?

(A) $2.06
(B) $2.19
(C) $3.00
(D) $4.30
(E) $6.45

5. Ⓐ Ⓑ Ⓒ Ⓓ Ⓔ

6. Ⓐ Ⓑ Ⓒ Ⓓ Ⓔ

Answer #5: Ⓓ

Formula: • Rate $= \dfrac{\text{Amount}}{\text{Time}}$

Concept: • Rates

There are many ways to approach this problem. One method is to set up the equivalence, "4 minutes is to 24¢ as 15 minutes is to x¢." As an equation, this looks like:

$$\frac{4 \text{ minutes}}{24¢} = \frac{15 \text{ minutes}}{x¢}$$

Cross multiplying and then solving for x you get:

$4x = 24 \times 15$

$x = 6 \times 15$

$x = 90¢$

Notice that by factoring out common divisors you can reduce the size of your numbers before multiplying. This helps reduce the chance of error.

Answer #6: Ⓑ

Formula: • In a sequence that repeats after n items, every item whose position is divisible by n will be the same as the nth item.

Concept: • Repeating sequences☆

The first person pays 15¢ and wins a penny, so the booth earns 14¢. The second person pays 15¢ and wins a nickel, so the booth earns 10¢. Likewise, the booth earns 5¢ from the third person and loses 10¢ from the fourth person. Then the cycle repeats. So each cycle through the game, the booth earns: 14¢ + 10¢ + 5¢ − 10¢ = 19¢.

The problem asks for how much money is made after 43 people have played the game. 43 is not divisible by 4 so let's look at the 40th person, the previous number divisible by 4. After the 40th person has played, the booth has been through 10 complete cycle. Having earned 19¢ per cycle, the booth has netted \$1.90 profit. The booth earns 14¢ off the 41st player, bringing the profit to \$2.04, then 10¢ and 5¢ from the 42nd and 43rd players, bringing the total profit to \$2.19.

☆ See Concept-to-Problem Index page 141.

7. If $x - y = 10$, then
   $x - (2 - y) =$

   (A) 8
   (B) 10
   (C) 12
   (D) 18
   (E) cannot be determined

A is the set of integers evenly
    divisible by 2.
B is the set of integers evenly
    divisible by 3.
C is the set of integers evenly
    divisible by 6.

8. Which of the following numbers is contained within the
   intersection of A, B, and C?

   (A) 220
   (B) 221
   (C) 222
   (D) 224
   (E) 225

7. Ⓐ Ⓑ Ⓒ Ⓓ Ⓔ

8. Ⓐ Ⓑ Ⓒ Ⓓ Ⓔ

Answer #7:   Ⓔ
Formula: • $a - (b - c) = a - b + c$.
Concepts: • Arithmetic
  • Pick and chooses$^{☆}$

Every SAT I've ever seen has at least one question that tests your ability to remove parentheses preceded by a subtraction sign. In this case, $x - (2 - y) = x - 2 + y$.

From $x - y = 10$, you know nothing about $x + y$, so you can't simplify the second expression.

If you're not sure that an answer can't be determined, try picking numbers that satisfy the first equation. If they yield different values in the second equation you are guaranteed that "cannot be determined" is the correct answer.

For example, let x be 10 and y be 0. This clearly satisfies the first equation. Plugging these values into the second equation yields $10 - (2 - 0) = 8$. Now let x be 11 and y be 1. These values also satisfy the first equation. However, they yield $11 - (2 - 1) = 10$ for the value of the second equation.

Because two sets of numbers that satisfy the first equation yield different values for the second equation, there is no fixed value for the second expression.

Answer #8:   Ⓒ
Theorems: • All numbers divisible by 2 end in either 0, 2, 4, 6, or 8.
  If a number is divisible by 3, then the sum of its digits is divisible by 3.
Concepts: • Factoring and prime factors
  • Arithmetic

Answers B and E end in 1 and 5, respectively, so they are not divisible by 2, not in set A, and consequently not in the intersection of the three sets.

The digits of answers A and D add up to 4 and 8, respectively. Neither of these is divisible by 3, so they are not in set B and consequently not in the intersection of sets A, B, and C.

We know that 222 is in set A because it ends in a 2 and therefore is divisible by 2. We know that 222 is in set B because the sum of its digits is 6, which is divisible by 3. Finally, we know that 222 is in set C because any number divisible by both 2 and 3 is divisible by 6.

9. 30% of 80 is what percent of 24?

  (A) 44
  (B) 50
  (C) 56
  (D) 66
  (E) 100

10. Because of bad weather, a traveler could average 40 miles per hour during a 240-mile trip from city A to city B. Coming back, she was able to average 60 miles per hour. What was her overall average speed measured in miles per hour?

  (A) 45
  (B) 48
  (C) 50
  (D) 52
  (E) 55

9. (A) (B) (C) (D) (E)

10. (A) (B) (C) (D) (E)

Answer #9:   (E)

Formula: • $x\%$ of $y = \dfrac{x}{100}\,y$

Concepts: • Percentages
              • Word problems

Because this is a word problem, your first step is to convert it to an equation. This is most easily done phrase by phrase:

You read:	*You write:*
1. 30% of 80	$\dfrac{30}{100} \times 80$
2. is	$\dfrac{30}{100} \times 80 =$
3. what percent	$\dfrac{30}{100} \times 80 = \dfrac{p}{100}$
4. of 24	$\dfrac{30}{100} \times 80 = \dfrac{p}{100} \times 24$

Now solve for p. Before doing any arithmetic, it's helpful to cancel out the 100s on both sides of the equal sign. This leaves you with $30 \times 80 = p \times 24$. Because $3 \times 8 = 24$, you next want to expand the left side of the equation to read:

$$3 \times 10 \times 8 \times 10 = p \times 24$$

Then you divide 24 out from both sides of the equation to end up with $10 \times 10 = p$, or $p = 100$.

Answer #10:   (B)

Formula: • Rate $= \dfrac{\text{Amount}}{\text{Time}}$

Concept: • Rates

Rates can be tricky. If you drive 50 mph for an hour and 60 mph for an hour your average is 55 mph during the 2 hours. However, if you drive 50 mph for 30 miles and 60 mph for 30 miles, your average is NOT 55 mph. Why not? Because it took you longer to drive the first 30 miles.

In this problem, the woman drove 240 miles at 40 mph. This took her $\dfrac{240}{40} = 6$ hrs. Then the woman drove another 240 miles at 60 mph. This took her $\dfrac{240}{60} = 4$ hrs. The total time she spent driving was 6 hrs + 4 hrs = 10 hrs. The total distance she drove was 240 miles × 2 = 480 miles. So her average miles per hour was $\dfrac{480 \text{ miles}}{10 \text{ hours}} = 48$ mph.

11. If $x^2 + y^2 = 15$, and $xy = 5$, then $x + y =$

(A) 5 only
(B) −5 only
(C) 5 or −5
(D) 5 or 10
(E) 10 or −10

12. A woman jogs 6 miles at 4 miles per hour. At *approximately* what speed would she need to travel during the next $2\frac{1}{2}$ hours to have an average speed of 6 miles per hour during the complete trip?

(A) 4 mph
(B) 6 mph
(C) 7 mph
(D) 9 mph
(E) 10 mph

11. Ⓐ Ⓑ Ⓒ Ⓓ Ⓔ

12. Ⓐ Ⓑ Ⓒ Ⓓ Ⓔ

Answer #11: Ⓒ

Formulas:
- $(x + y)^2 = x^2 + 2xy + y^2$
- If $x^2 = y$, then $x = \sqrt{y}$ or $x = -\sqrt{y}$

Concept:
- Polynomial arithmetic

As you start this problem, if you notice that the question is asking for the value of $x + y$ and you notice that you have many of the components for determining the value of $(x + y)^2$, then you're on the right track. By reordering its terms, you can say that:

$$(x + y)^2 = x^2 + 2xy + y^2$$
$$= x^2 + y^2 + 2xy$$

Because you know that $x^2 + y^2 = 15$ and that $xy = 5$, you can substitute into your equation to get:

$$(x + y)^2 = 15 + 2(5)$$
$$= 25$$

Remember that every positive number has two square roots, a positive one and a negative one. In this case, $25 = (-5)^2 = (5)^2$. So, there are two possible values for $(x + y)$, −5, and 5.

Answer #12: Ⓒ

Formula:
- $\text{Rate} = \dfrac{\text{Amount}}{\text{Time}}$

Concepts:
- Rates
- Approximation ☆

This problem breaks the woman's jog into two parts and gives you data about each part. Each time you know two out of three parameters in the rate equation. You must apply the equation to the different jog parts and to the whole, until you can solve for the rate at which the woman travels during the second part, Rate_2. Each of the following steps computes a missing piece.

You are told:
- $\text{Dist}_1 = 6$ miles
- $\text{Rate}_1 = 4$ mph
- $\text{Time}_2 = 2.5$ hours
- $\text{Rate}_w = 6$ mph

You compute:
- $\text{Time}_1 = \text{Dist}_1 \div \text{Rate}_1 = 6$ miles $\div$ 4 mph = 1.5 hrs
- $\text{Time}_w = \text{Time}_1 + \text{Time}_2 = 1.5$ hrs + 2.5 hrs = 4 hrs
- $\text{Dist}_w = \text{Rate}_w \times \text{Time}_w = 6$ mph $\times$ 4 hrs = 24 miles
- $\text{Dist}_2 = \text{Dist}_w - \text{Dist}_1 = 24$ miles − 6 miles = 18 miles
- $\text{Rate}_2 = \text{Dist}_2 \div \text{Time}_2 = 18$ miles $\div$ 2.5 hrs = 7.2 mph

Because the problem asks for an approximate speed, you should round 7.2 to 7.

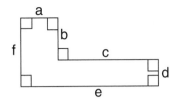

13. The area of the above figure is all of the following *except*:

(A) $ab + de$
(B) $af + cd$
(C) $fe - bc$
(D) $af + de$
(E) $ab + ad + cd$

14. If $(x - 2)(x + 2) = (x - 2)^2$, then $x =$

(A) -4
(B) -2
(C) 0
(D) 2
(E) 4

13. (A) (B) (C) (D) (E)

14. (A) (B) (C) (D) (E)

Answer #13: Ⓓ

Formula: • Area of a Rectangle = Length × Width
Concept: • Rectangle geometry

The possible solutions to the problem all make use of the rectangles that make up the larger picture. This suggests that you should explicitly draw in those rectangles:

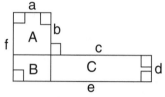

Now you can see more clearly that the total area of the figure is A + B + C. The first offered solution is *ab* + *de*. *ab* = A, and *de* = B + C, so *ab* + *de* = A + B + C, the total area of the figure. Continuing in this same fashion, all of the expressions in the possible solutions are equal to the area of the figure except D. Solution D is *af* + *ed*. *af* = A + B and *ed* = B + C, so *af* + *ed* = A + B + B + C. The rectangle with area B is counted twice; therefore, *af* + *de* is greater than, not equal to, the area of the original figure.

Answer #14: Ⓓ

Formula: • Division by 0 is undefined
Concept: • Polynomial arithmetic

When you first see this problem, you might notice that there's an (x −2) on both sides of the equation and divide it out, leaving: x + 2 = x − 2. Further simplifying what's left by subtracting an x from both sides you get 2 = − 2. Oops! In almost every case, this one included, if after doing a division you come up with one number equal to a different one, then you divided by zero.

In this case, because division by zero is not defined, when you divide both sides of the equation by (x − 2) you must consider the case that x = 2 (i.e. x − 2 = 0). The simplest way to consider this case is to plug 2 in for x and see if you get a true statement. Plugging 2 in for x leaves you (0)(4) = 0, which is a true statement. So 2 is the correct solution.

15. The operation $\boxed{x}$ indicates that one should subtract 2 from x and then multiply the result by 2. The operation $\widehat{x}$ indicates that one should multiply x by 2 and then subtract 2 from the product. Therefore, $\widehat{x} - \boxed{x} =$

(A) −2
(B) 0
(C) 2
(D) 4
(E) cannot be determined from the given information

16. Joan can paint m meters of fence in h hours and 15 minutes. What is her average speed in meters per hour?

(A) $h\left(1 + \dfrac{1}{4}\right)m$

(B) $\dfrac{m}{h + 15}$

(C) $\dfrac{4m}{4h + 1}$

(D) $\dfrac{h + 15}{m}$

(E) $\dfrac{h + \dfrac{1}{4}}{m}$

15. Ⓐ Ⓑ Ⓒ Ⓓ Ⓔ

16. Ⓐ Ⓑ Ⓒ Ⓓ Ⓔ

Answer #15: Ⓒ

Formula: • $a - b(c - d) = a - bc + bd$
Concepts: • Arithmetic
              • Functions
              • Word problems

Both ⏍ and ⊗ are described in words. Your first step is to translate the words to mathematical expressions. To determine the value of ⏍, as noted, you "subtract 2 and then multiply the result by 2." As a mathematical expression this can be written ⏍ $= 2(x - 2)$. Likewise, to determine the value of ⊗, you "multiply by 2 and then subtract 2 from the product." As a mathematical expression, this can be written: ⊗ $= (2x - 2)$.

Now, ⊗ − ⏍ can be written $(2x - 2) - 2(x - 2)$. Simplifying this expression, you get $2x - 2 - 2x + 4$ which is 2, answer C.

When removing the second set of parentheses, don't forget to change the sign on the last 2 and to multiply both the x and the 2 inside the parentheses by the 2 outside of the parentheses. These are both common errors. In fact, they are the skills that you are being tested on in this problem.

Answer #16: Ⓒ

Formulas: • 1 hour = 60 minutes
              • Rate $= \dfrac{\text{Amount}}{\text{Time}}$
Concepts: • Unit conversions ☆
              • Fractions
              • Rates

Because this problem asks for Joan's average speed in meters per hour, we know that we should convert the 15 minutes to 0.25 hours. The problem asks for the average painting rate so you need to divide the total length of fence, m meters, by the total time, $h + 0.25$ hours, to get $\dfrac{m}{h + 0.25}$. Although this is correct, it isn't one of the answer choices!

Before dismissing your solution, try simplifying it. Get rid of the 0.25 in the denominator of the fraction by multiplying top and bottom by 4. The result is $\dfrac{4m}{4h + 1}$.

17. If a woman is paid c dollars an hour for every hour she works up to eight hours and is paid double for every hour she works after eight hours, how many dollars will she be paid for working h hours, where $h > 8$?

(A) ch

(B) $\dfrac{h}{c}$

(C) $2ch - 8c$

(D) $ch + 8c$

(E) $2ch + 8$

18. If $x > y$ then the point (x,y) can be in all of the following areas of the coordinate axes *except:*

(A) Quadrant I
(B) Quadrant II
(C) Quadrant III
(D) Quadrant IV
(E) The x or y axes

17. Ⓐ Ⓑ Ⓒ Ⓓ Ⓔ

18. Ⓐ Ⓑ Ⓒ Ⓓ Ⓔ

Answer #17: Ⓒ

Formula: • $ = hours × rate
Concept: • Rates

This problem tests your ability to apply two salary rates. Because the total number of hours the woman worked, h, is greater than 8, she works the full 8 hours at the lower salary rate. How many hours does she work at the higher rate? She has worked a total of h hours, 8 of them at the lower salary rate, so the rest, $(h - 8)$, must be at the higher rate.

Now you know the amounts of time and the rates at which the woman worked, so you can apply the rate formula to determine how much she earned:

Total earnings = earnings during first 8 hrs.
                    + earnings for work after 8 hrs
                  = 8 times lower rate
                    + $(h - 8)$ times higher rate
                  = $8c + (h - 8)2c$
                  = $8c + 2ch - 16c$
                  = $2ch - 8c$

Answer #18: Ⓑ

Definitions: • Quadrant
                    • Coordinate axes
Concept: • Coordinate geometry

This is a good situation in which to draw a picture. The coordinate axes can be drawn as follows:

Now, add the line $y = x$. It's a line running diagonally from the lower left of the graph to the upper right at a 45° angle to the axes. Next, shade in the area of the graph to the right and below the line. This is the area in which $x > y$. The only quadrant with no shading is Quadrant II, answer B.

Another way of looking at this problem is to say that in Quadrant II x is always negative and y is always positive. No negative number is greater than any positive number; so, in Quadrant II x can never be greater than y.

19. $\triangle ABC$ has angles of $30°$, $45°$, and $105°$. If the side opposite the $30°$ angle has length $\sqrt{2}$, then the area of $\triangle ABC$ is:

   (A) $\dfrac{1}{2} + \dfrac{\sqrt{3}}{2}$

   (B) $2\sqrt{2}$

   (C) $1 + \sqrt{3}$

   (D) $\dfrac{1}{2} + \dfrac{\sqrt{6}}{2}$

   (E) $\dfrac{\sqrt{2}}{2} + \sqrt{3}$

20. Over what interval(s) is the statement $x^3 < x^2$ true?

   (A) all x
   (B) $x > 0$
   (C) $x > 1$ or $x < -1$
   (D) $-1 < x < 1$
   (E) $x > 1$

19. Ⓐ Ⓑ Ⓒ Ⓓ Ⓔ

20. Ⓐ Ⓑ Ⓒ Ⓓ Ⓔ

Answer #19: Ⓐ

Definitions:
- In a 30-60-90 triangle, the lengths of the sides opposite the angles are in the ratio of $1 : \sqrt{3} : 2$
- In a 45-45-90 triangle, the lengths of the sides opposite the angles are in the ratio of $1 : 1 : \sqrt{2}$

Concept:
- Triangle geometry

The first step in solving this problem is to draw the picture:

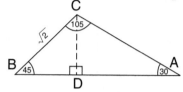

Now draw the perpendicular from C to $\overline{AB}$ and notice that you get a 45-45-90 and a 30-60-90 triangle.

Next, using the formula for 45-45-90 triangles, you can compute the lengths of $\overline{CD}$ and $\overline{BD}$, which are both 1.

Write these in. Using the formula for 30-60-90 triangles, you can see that the length of $\overline{AD}$ is $\sqrt{3}$.

The altitude of the triangle is 1 and the base is $1 + \sqrt{3}$. It follows that the area $\triangle ABC$ is $\dfrac{1}{2} + \dfrac{\sqrt{3}}{2}$, answer A.

Answer #20: Ⓔ

Formula:
- x^2 is non-negative for all x

Concepts:
- Exponents
- Inequalities

You are being asked to solve the inequality $x^3 > x^2$.

Subtract x^2 from both sides: $x^3 - x^2 > 0$

Factor an x^2 out on the left: $x^2(x - 1) > 0$

Note that x cannot be 0 because the statement $x^3 < x^2$ is not true when x is 0. Also, x^2 is never negative, so you can divide both sides of the inequality by x^2 without having to worry about changing the direction of the inequality sign.

Divide both sides of the inequality by x^2: $x - 1 > 0$

Add 1 to both sides: $x > 1$

21. A six-sided, fair die is rolled 100 times. Which of the following statements must be true?

 I. At least one side lands face up at least 17 times.
 II. All sides land face up at least 16 times.
 III. Side one lands face up at least 2 times.

(A) None is true
(B) I only
(C) II only
(D) III only
(E) All are true

22. The sum of the squares of integers from 1 to n is equal to $\frac{1}{6}n(n + 1)(2n + 1)$. What is the average of the set of squares $\{1^2, 2^2, \ldots, 9^2\}$?

(A) 31

(B) $\dfrac{95}{3}$

(C) $\dfrac{95}{2}$

(D) 190

(E) 285

21. Ⓐ Ⓑ Ⓒ Ⓓ Ⓔ

22. Ⓐ Ⓑ Ⓒ Ⓓ Ⓔ

Answer #21:   Ⓑ

Concept: • Probability

Probability problems on the SAT often test your ability to distinguish between valid and faulty statements. Usually, instead of calculating solutions, you will solve problems by creating examples of low probability situations that disprove statements. These situations often consist of one event happening every time or every event happening evenly.

In this problem you can create the situation that, as improbable as it might be, the die lands on side six every time. From this example you can immediately disprove statements II and III.

To disprove statement I you want to create a situation wherein each side of the die comes up no more than 16 times. If each side of a six-sided die lands face up 16 times, the die must have been rolled 6 × 16 = 96 times. Yet the die in the problem was rolled 100 times. These last four rolls must land on some side and that side has landed up at least 17 times; therefore, statement I is true, and it is the only one that is true.

Answer #22:   Ⓑ

Definition: • Average $= \dfrac{\text{Sum of the items in a list}}{\text{Number of items in the list}}$

Concept: • Averages

For this problem you're asked to find the average of the set of squares, n^2, for n from 1 to 9.

You're told that the sum of these numbers can be computed with the formula $\dfrac{1}{6}n(n + 1)(2n + 1)$. In this case, n is nine so you can write the sum as $\dfrac{1}{6}(9)(10)(19)$. You also know that there are 9 integers between 1 and 9 inclusive. So, you've got all of the pieces to compute the average:

$$Average = \frac{\frac{1}{6}(9)(10)(19)}{9}$$

$$= \frac{1}{6}(10)(19)$$

$$= \frac{190}{6}$$

$$= \frac{95}{3}$$

23. A square is inscribed in a circle in such a way that the vertices of the square touch the circle. If the square has side $a\sqrt{2}$, then the area of the circle is:

(A) $\dfrac{1}{4}\pi a^2$

(B) $\dfrac{1}{2}\pi a^2$

(C) πa^2

(D) $\sqrt{2}\pi a^2$

(E) $2\pi a^2$

24. A group of 9 friends invest equally in a business opportunity that costs $20,000. If n more friends were to take part evenly in the investment, which expression best describes how much less each of the original 9 would have to pay?

(A) $\dfrac{20{,}000}{9} - \dfrac{20{,}000}{n}$

(B) $\dfrac{20{,}000}{9} - \dfrac{20{,}000}{9+n}$

(C) $\dfrac{20{,}000}{9+n}$

(D) $\dfrac{20{,}000}{n}$

(E) $\dfrac{20{,}000}{9-n}$

23. Ⓐ Ⓑ Ⓒ Ⓓ Ⓔ

24. Ⓐ Ⓑ Ⓒ Ⓓ Ⓔ

Answer #23: Ⓒ

Formulas: • The length of the diagonal of a square with side s is $s\sqrt{2}$
                   • Area of a circle = πr^2

Concepts: • Circle geometry
                   • Rectangle geometry

Start with a picture:

For this problem, begin with the fact that the square has side $a\sqrt{2}$ and compute the length of its diagonal:

$a\sqrt{2}\sqrt{2} = 2a$. Notice that the diagonals of the square are also diameters of the circle. The radius of the circle is half its diameter so you can compute it to be a. Given the radius of the circle, you can compute the area of the circle: $A = \pi r^2 = \pi a^2$, answer C.

Answer #24: Ⓑ

Concept: • Word Problems

This problem type tests your ability to model a situation with mathematical expressions. Notice that you never have to do the arithmetic. To start this problem look at what's being asked for: "how much less each . . . would pay." How much less they would pay is the difference between what they would pay before and after the additional friends joined in.

Before the additional friends joined in, each friend had to pay one ninth of the $20,000 cost, or $\dfrac{20,000}{9}$ dollars. With the additional friends there are $9 + n$ people, so each person must pay $\dfrac{1}{9+n}$ of the $20,000, or $\dfrac{20,000}{9+n}$ dollars. The difference between the cost before and after is, therefore, answer B: $\dfrac{20,000}{9} - \dfrac{20,000}{9+n}$.

25. If $.2^2 = \sqrt{x}$, then $x =$

    (A) .2
    (B) .02
    (C) .04
    (D) .016
    (E) .0016

25. Ⓐ   Ⓑ   Ⓒ   Ⓓ   Ⓔ

Answer #25: (E)

Concepts: • Arithmetic
                 • Exponents and square roots

This problem has two twists. First, the question mixes a square root, $\sqrt{x}$, and a square, $.2^2$. Many people, in a hurry, will toss out the exponent and the radical sign to get $.2 = x$, which is incorrect.

The second twist is raising a decimal to a power. Moving too quickly you might write $.2^2 = .4$. It's often easier to do arithmetic with fractions: $.2 = \dfrac{2}{10}$ and $.2^2 = \left(\dfrac{2}{10}\right)^2 = \dfrac{4}{100}$.

Squaring both sides of the original equation you get:

$$x = (.2^2)^2 = .2^4 = \left(\dfrac{2}{10}\right)^4 = \dfrac{16}{10^4} = .0016, \text{ answer E.}$$

SECTION 2

Questions 26–40 each consist of two quantities, one in Column A and one in Column B. You are to compare the two quantities and on the answer sheet fill in:

A   if the quantity in Column A is greater
B   if the quantity in Column B is greater
C   if the two quantities are equal
D   if the relationship cannot be determined from the information given
AN E RESPONSE WILL NOT BE SCORED

NOTES:

1. In certain questions, information concerning one or both of the quantities to be compared is centered above the two columns.
2. In a given question, a symbol that appears in both columns represents the same thing in Column A as it does in Column B.
3. Letters such as x, n, and k stand for real numbers.

	EXAMPLES	
	Column A	Column B
E1.	2×6	$2 + 6$

	Column A	Column B
E2.	$180 - x$	y
E3.	$p - q$	$q - p$

E1. ● Ⓑ Ⓒ Ⓓ
E2. Ⓐ Ⓑ ● Ⓓ
E3. Ⓐ Ⓑ Ⓒ ●

26.

27.

$$y^2 = 36$$
$$x^2 = 25$$

Column A	Column B
The number of prime numbers between 1 and 100	The number of odd numbers between 1 and 100

Column A	Column B
x	y

26. Ⓐ Ⓑ Ⓒ Ⓓ

27. Ⓐ Ⓑ Ⓒ Ⓓ

Answer #26: (B)

Definitions: • Odd number: A number not divisible by 2
                   • Prime number: A number only divisible by 1 and itself

Concept: • Factoring and prime numbers

All primes (except 2) are odd. Many odd numbers, such as 9, 15, 21, and 25, are not prime, so there are many more odd numbers than primes between 1 and 100.

Answer #27: (D)

Concept: • Exponents and square roots

This problem tests whether you know that for most second degree equations—those with a variable raised to the power of 2—there are two solutions. In the first equation, $y^2 = 36$, the two solutions are $y = 6$ or $y = -6$.

   If in this problem $y = 6$ and $x = -5$, then y $>$ x. But if $y = -6$ and $x = 5$, then $x > y$. Consequently, you cannot determine the relationship between x and y for all cases, so the answer is D.

28.

29.

$$x = 1 - \cfrac{1}{1 - \cfrac{1}{2}}$$

Column A	Column B		Column A	Column B
32	8.2×4.3		x	$\dfrac{1}{2}$

28. Ⓐ Ⓑ Ⓒ Ⓓ

29. Ⓐ Ⓑ Ⓒ Ⓓ

Answer #28: Ⓑ

Concepts: • Approximation☆
  • Arithmetic

Being able to look at an arithmetic expression and have a rough idea of the answer is an important skill. This problem tests your ability to look at the expression 8.2 × 4.3 and notice quickly that it is a little more than 32.

How? You should recognize that 8 × 4 = 32. You also know that 8.2 is a little more than 8, and 4.3 is a little more than 4, so their product is a little more than 8 × 4 or 32. Notice that we never had to do the arithmetic or take the chance of making a multiplication error.

Now that the SAT allows you to use calculators you could have multiplied 8.2 and 4.3 using a calculator and compared the result (35.26) to 32. However, that also has the potential for error and probably isn't any faster than approximating.

Answer #29: Ⓑ

Definitions: • The reciprocal of x is $\dfrac{1}{x}$

  • $\dfrac{1}{a/b} = \dfrac{b}{a}$

Concept: • Fractions

Doing this problem one step at a time only involves knowing what $1 - \dfrac{1}{2}$ is (easy enough!) and how to compute the reciprocal of a fraction.

First, simplify the denominator of the larger fraction from $1 - \dfrac{1}{2}$ to just $\dfrac{1}{2}$. Now you're left with the equation $x = 1 - \dfrac{1}{1/2}$. If you know that the reciprocal of a fraction can be computed by "flipping over" the fraction, then you know that $\dfrac{1}{1/2} = 2$, and, consequently, you can further simplify the equation to read $x = 1 - 2$. Now finish solving to get $x = -1$. Column A, −1, is less than $\dfrac{1}{2}$, so the answer is B.

☆ See Concept-to-Problem Index page 139.

30.

Five years ago blue ribbon cost 20¢ more per yard than red ribbon.

Column A	Column B
The cost of red ribbon now	The cost of blue ribbon now

31.

Column A	Column B
The sum of the remainders when 5 is divided into five consecutive numbers	5

30. (A) (B) (C) (D)

31. (A) (B) (C) (D)

Answer #30: Ⓓ

Concept: • Irrelevant information☆

Knowing how to spot irrelevant information is one of several skills tested on the SAT.

    In this example, knowing the price of red and blue ribbon from five years ago tells you nothing about the price now. Maybe the cost of red dye skyrocketed; maybe neither price changed. In short, from the information given, you do not know the relationship between the cost of red ribbon now (Column A) and the cost of blue ribbon now (Column B), so the correct answer is D.

Answer #31: Ⓐ

Definition: • Remainder
Concept: • Arithmetic

Remainders have a lot of interesting properties. For example, when 5 is divided into a number, the possible remainders are 0, 1, 2, 3, or 4. Furthermore, if 5 is divided into a number and has a remainder of 3, then the remainder when 5 is divided into the next number is 4, and 5 will evenly divide the number after that (i.e., the remainder is 0).

    For this problem, you need to know that if 5 is divided into any five consecutive numbers then the set of remainders must be 0, 1, 2, 3, and 4. Without doing the addition, you should notice that the sum of these numbers is greater than 5. Why? The set includes a 4 and a 3. The 4 and 3 add up to 7, which is greater than 5, so adding even more positive numbers only increases the total. Consequently, the value described in Column A is greater than 5, the value in Column B.

    As is often the case, by looking at the problem carefully before performing computations, you can often avoid doing arithmetic altogether and the possibility for miscalculation that goes along with it.

32.

n is a positive integer

Column A	Column B
$(-1)^n$	1^n

33.

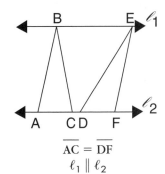

$$\overline{AC} = \overline{DF}$$
$$\ell_1 \parallel \ell_2$$

Column A	Column B
Area of $\triangle ABC$	Area of $\triangle DEF$

---

32. Ⓐ Ⓑ Ⓒ Ⓓ

33. Ⓐ Ⓑ Ⓒ Ⓓ

Answer #32: Ⓓ

Formulas:
- $(-1)^n = 1$, if n is an even number
- $= -1$, if n is an odd number

Concept:
- Exponents

Problems that involve raising −1 and 1 to powers occur often on the SAT because, unlike other numbers, −1 or 1 raised to a power is always 1 or −1.

The value in Column B, 1^n, equals 1 for every integer n. The value in Column A, $(-1)^n$, equals −1 if n is odd and 1 if n is even. In one case, the values in the two columns are equal; in the other case, the value in column B is greater. Because the only restriction on n is that it is positive, not that it is odd or even, you can't tell which case holds and therefore can't determine the relationship between the values in the two columns.

Answer #33: Ⓒ

Formulas:
- Area of a triangle $= \dfrac{1}{2} \times$ base $\times$ height
- The distance between parallel lines is the same at every point along the lines

Concept:
- Triangle geometry

Your goal is to determine the relationship between the areas of the two triangles ABC and DEF. If you can show that the corresponding bases and heights of the two triangles are equal, then you have shown that their areas are also equal.

You are given the fact that $\overline{AC} = \overline{DF}$, so you know the bases of $\triangle ABC$ and $\triangle DEF$ are equal. The corresponding altitudes to these bases are the perpendiculars between ℓ_1 and ℓ_2 that pass through points B and E. Because ℓ_1 and ℓ_2 are parallel, you know that the distance between them is the same wherever it is measured. Consequently, the altitudes of the two triangles are also equal.

Because both the bases and the altitudes of the two triangles are equal their areas must also be equal, so the correct answer is C.

34. Let $\boxed{n}$ be defined by the equation $\boxed{n} = (n + 1)^2$

35.

Column A	Column B
$\dfrac{\boxed{8}}{\boxed{4}}$	$\boxed{2}$

Column A	Column B
$a\%$ of b	$b\%$ of a

34. Ⓐ Ⓑ Ⓒ Ⓓ

35. Ⓐ Ⓑ Ⓒ Ⓓ

Answer #34: Ⓑ

Concept: • Functions

In this problem, the fraction on the left becomes:
$\frac{(8 + 1)^2}{(4 + 1)^2}$. You can simplify this to be $\frac{9^2}{5^2}$, and further simplify it to be $\left(\frac{9}{5}\right)^2$.
   Before reducing Column A any further, look at Column B, which simplifies to $\boxed{2}$ = $(2 + 1)^2$ = $(3)^2$. Now you have $\left(\frac{9}{5}\right)^2$ in Column A and 3^2 in Column B. $\frac{9}{5}$ is pretty close to 2, so without doing any arithmetic you know that $\frac{9}{5} < 3$ and consequently $\left(\frac{9}{5}\right)^2 < 3^2$. Therefore, the value in Column B is greater than Column A.

Answer #35: Ⓒ

Formula: • $x\% = \dfrac{x}{100}$

Concept: • Percentages

You've probably been told many times that a percentage is shorthand for a fraction whose denominator is 100. So, "$x\%$ of something" is shorthand for saying $\dfrac{x}{100}$ multiplied by that thing.

   Given this definition, we can rewrite "$a\%$ of b" from Column A as $\dfrac{a}{100} \times b$ = $\dfrac{ab}{100}$. We can also rewrite "$b\%$ of a" from Column B as $\dfrac{b}{100} \times a = \dfrac{ba}{100}$. Because multiplication is commutative—that is, $ab = ba$—we know that $\dfrac{ab}{100} = \dfrac{ba}{100}$. Therefore, the values in Columns A and B are equal for any a and b, and the correct answer is C.

36.

37.

$$t < s$$

Column A	Column B
The average of t and s	s

Column A	Column B
The distance from the point (a, a) to the point (x, y) on the coordinate axes	The distance from the point (a, a) to the point (y, x) on the coordinate axes

36. Ⓐ Ⓑ Ⓒ Ⓓ

37. Ⓐ Ⓑ Ⓒ Ⓓ

Answer #36: Ⓑ

Definition: • Average = $\dfrac{\text{sum of the items in a list}}{\text{number of items in the list}}$

Concept: • Averages

Given any two unequal numbers, their average has to be somewhere between them. Therefore, the average of t and s lies somewhere between t and s. Because t is less than s, you know that any number between t and s is less than s. Therefore, the value described in column B is greater than the value in Column A.

Answer #37: Ⓒ

Formula: • The distance between two points (x_1, y_1) and (x_2, y_2) is $\sqrt{(x_2 - x_1)^2 + (y_2 - y_1)^2}$

Concept: • Coordinate geometry

To determine the value described in Column A, plug (a,a) for (x_1, y_1) and (x,y) for (x_2, y_2) into the distance equation to get $\sqrt{(x - a)2^2 + (y - a)^2}$. Likewise, to determine the value described in Column B, plug in (a,a) for (x_1, y_1) and (y,x) for (x_2, y_2) to get $\sqrt{(y - a)^2 + (x - a)^2}$. The only difference between the two expressions is the order in which $(y - a)^2$ and $(x - a)^2$ are added. Because order doesn't matter when adding integers, you know that the two expressions are equal.

38.

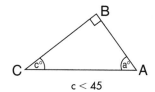

c < 45

Column A	Column B
The length of	The length of
$\overline{AB}$	$\overline{CB}$

39.

$$a > b + 1$$

Column A	Column B
a	b

38. Ⓐ Ⓑ Ⓒ Ⓓ

39. Ⓐ Ⓑ Ⓒ Ⓓ

Answer #38: Ⓑ

Theorems: • If X and Y are the sides of a triangle, and x and y are the opposite angles, it follows that:
1) if $x > y$, then $X > Y$
2) if $X > Y$, then $x > y$
• The sum of the angles of a triangle is $180°$

Concept: • Triangle geometry

The sum of the angle measures in a triangle is always $180°$. Therefore, if you subtract the $90°$ indicated by the small square at vertex B, you are left with $a° + c° = 90°$.

In the problem definition you are told that $c < 45$. From this and the fact that $a + c = 90$, you can deduce that $a > 45$. Even though you don't know what a and c are, you can write their relationship as $a > 45 > c$.

Because angle A is greater than angle C, the side opposite angle A, $\overline{BC}$, is longer than the side opposite angle C, $\overline{AB}$. Hence, the value in Column B is greater than the value in Column A, and the correct answer is B.

Answer #39: Ⓐ

Concept: • Inequalities

Problems like this occur on the SAT more to ensure that you are careful than to test some specific skill. The problem definition tells you that $a > b + 1$. You know that $b + 1 > b$, so you can write the relation between a and b as $a > b + 1 > b$.

Now you can read off the answer: The value in Column A, a, is greater than the value in Column B, b.

Note that if you were told $a < b + 1$, you couldn't ascertain the relationship between a and b because a might be a lot less than $b + 1$, in which case it would also be less than b, or it might be between b and $b + 1$, in which case $a > b$.

40.

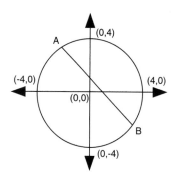

Column A	Column B
The length of $\overline{AB}$	8

40. (A) (B) (C) (D)

Answer #40: Ⓑ

Theorem:	• The diameter of the circle is the longest chord of the circle
Concept:	• Circle geometry

$\overline{AB}$ is a chord of the circle but it's not the diameter, so its length must be less than the diameter of the circle. The diameter of the circle is the distance from (0,4) to (0, −4), which, by inspection, you can calculate to be 8. Therefore, $\overline{AB}$ is less than 8 and the value of Column A is less than the value of Column B.

TEST 1

SECTION 3

This section of the test requires you to enter your solution to each of the following ten problems onto a grid. The grid consists of four columns and twelve rows. To enter a number onto the grid, write each of its digits or symbols, in order, in the boxes at the top of the grid. Then, shade in the corresponding box beneath it. A decimal point is provided for numbers such as .5, and a slash is provided for constructing fractions such as $\frac{1}{2}$. The following are examples of correctly entered numbers:

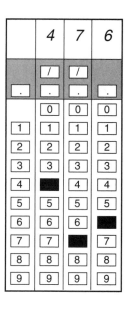
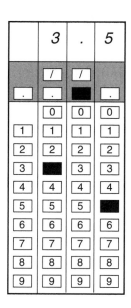
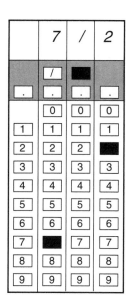

Remember the following when entering numbers onto the grid:

- Mark no more than one box in any one column.

- No question will have a negative answer.

- If your answer is a *fraction*, remember to grid-in the fraction line in its own column.

- If your answer contains a *decimal point*, you must enter it, too, in its own column.

- *Mixed numbers,* such as $3\frac{1}{2}$, must be gridded-in using decimals (i.e., 3.5) or as improper fractions (i.e., $\frac{7}{2}$). If you enter your answer as a mixed number, it will be incorrect. In the case of $3\frac{1}{2}$, the machine scoring your test will interpret 31/2 as $\frac{31}{2} = 15.5$.

- If the answer to a problem is a repeating decimal, such as .3333 . . . (or $.\overline{3}$), you may round your solution to the most accurate answer the grid can accommodate (i.e., .333). Less accurate values, such as .3, are incorrect.

41. If $x = 2y = 4z$ and $x + y + z = ay$, what is the value of a?

42. A desk and chair set costs $9.89. If a dozen sets are purchased as a group, the cost is reduced to $9.14 per set. A school needs to buy 123 sets. How many dollars does it save buying the sets by the dozen instead of individually?

41.

	/	/	
.	.	.	.
	0	0	0
1	1	1	1
2	2	2	2
3	3	3	3
4	4	4	4
5	5	5	5
6	6	6	6
7	7	7	7
8	8	8	8
9	9	9	9

42.

	/	/	
.	.	.	.
	0	0	0
1	1	1	1
2	2	2	2
3	3	3	3
4	4	4	4
5	5	5	5
6	6	6	6
7	7	7	7
8	8	8	8
9	9	9	9

Answer #41: 3.5 or $\dfrac{7}{2}$

Concept: • Solving equations

Looking at the right side of the second equation, ay, you can see that the important variable among x, y, and z is y. So, you'd like to rewrite the left side of that equation in terms of y. Using the first set of equations, you can replace every x in the second equation with $2y$. Likewise, you can replace every z in the second equation with $\dfrac{1}{2}y$. Doing these replacements in the second equation results in:

$$2y + y + \frac{1}{2}y = ay.$$

Now you can divide both sides of the equation by y to get

$$2 + 1 + \frac{1}{2} = a, \text{ or } 3\frac{1}{2} = a.$$

Warning: To grid in $3\dfrac{1}{2}$ you must write either "3.5" or "7/2." If you write "31/2" it will be misinterpreted as 15.5 and will be marked incorrect.*

Answer #42: 90

Concept: • Rates

For every set that the school buys as part of a dozen, it saves $9.89 − $9.14 = $.75 per desk-and-chair set. However, if you were to multiply $.75 by 123 sets, you'd be making a mistake. Remember that to receive the discounted price, the school must purchase 12 sets *as a group*. Ten groups of 12 sets is 120 sets; the last 3 sets must be purchased at the regular price. Therefore, the school saves:

$$.75 \frac{\$}{\text{set}} \times 120 \text{ sets} = \$90.$$

Note that when you grid in the 90, you do not add the dollar sign.*

---

* Gridded-in answers to these problems appear on page 137.

43.

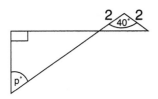

What is the value of p in the above figure?

44. If $(2^5 - 2^6)(2^0 - 2^1) = 2^x$, then what is the value of x?

Answer #43: 20

Theorems: • In a triangle, angles opposite equal sides are equal
                • Vertical angles are equal
                • The sum of the angle measures in a triangle is 180°
Concept: • Triangle geometry

By the time you have answered this problem, the diagram should be completely marked up. Start with it as it is presented and add information as you go. If you didn't mark up the figure, follow along now.

The unknown angles in the upper triangle are equal because they are opposite equal sides; draw an x in each one. Now you have three angles of a triangle, so their measures must sum to 180°. Write the equation $2x + 40 = 180$. Solving the equation for x you get $x = 70$. Replace the x's you wrote in with 70s. Because the two triangles share vertical angles and one of the angles is 70°, the other one must be, too. Write in 70° for the larger triangle's third angle measure. Now you have three angles listed for the larger triangle, 90°, 70°, and $p°$. They must sum to 180°, so you can set up the equation: $90 + 70 + p = 180$. Solving this equation, $p = 20$.*

Answer #44: 5
Formulas: • $a^{x+y} = a^x a^y$
                • If $a^x = a^y$, then $x = y$
Concepts: • Exponents
                • Arithmetic

With a fancier calculator you might be able to do this problem by brute force, calculating each of the values. A faster and less error-prone method is to factor the large exponents out of the expression $(2^5 - 2^6)$. The result of factoring 2^5 out of the first expression is:

$2^5(2^0 - 2^1)(2^0 - 2^1)$.

Any number raised to the 0th power is 1, and any number raised to the 1st power is itself, so you can further simplify the given equation to be $2^5(1 - 2)(1 - 2) = 2^x$. The two $(1 - 2)$'s both simplify to −1, and when multiplied together yield 1; further simplifying, you are left with $2^5 = 2^x$, which implies $x = 5$.*

---

* Gridded-in answers to these problems appear on page 137.

45.

What is a possible value for the length of $\overline{AB}$?

46.

Test #	% Correct
1	90
2	75
3	95
4	90
5	85

This table shows the percentage of questions Lynn answered correctly on each of five 60-question tests. What was the total number of questions Lynn answered correctly on the five tests?

45.

46.

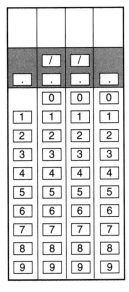

Answer #45: Any number n such that $2 < n < 4$

Concept: • Coordinate geometry

Not all math problems have exact solutions. With the inclusion of "grid-in" problems on the SAT, it is possible for people to give different answers to a problem and all be correct.

    To solve this particular problem, notice that A lies somewhere between -2 and -1 and B is somewhere between 1 and 2. The operative word here is *somewhere*. To maximize the length of $\overline{AB}$ you can imagine A right up against the -2 and B up against the 2; in this case, the length of $\overline{AB}$ would be infinitesimally less than 4. To minimize the length of $\overline{AB}$ you can imagine A right up against the -1 and B right up against the 1; in this case, the length of $\overline{AB}$ is infinitesimally greater than 2. Any number between 2 and 4, therefore, is a correct answer; note that 2 and 4 are *not* correct answers.*

Answer #46: 261

Formula: • $a\%$ of $b = \dfrac{a}{100} \times b$

Concept: • Tables and graphs
              • Percentages

This is another problem where writing on the test can help you keep your numbers straight and avoid arithmetic errors. 90% of 60 is $\dfrac{9}{10} \times 60 = 9 \times 6 = 54$. Write 54 to the right of each of 90% in the table. Similarly, 75% of 60 is 45, 95% of 60 is 57, and 85% of 60 is 51. Again, write each of these values in the table. Now you have a third column with the number of questions Lynn answered correctly for each test. Summing 54, 45, 57, 54, and 51 gives you the answer 261.*

---

* Gridded-in answers to these problems appear on page 138.

47.
$$N = \{2, 4, 6\}$$
$$D = \{3, 6, 9\}$$

What is the positive square root of the difference between the largest and smallest fractions that can be formed by choosing one number from set N to be the numerator and one number from set D to be the denominator?

48. It costs $18 to buy exactly enough paint to cover the surface of a solid cube. If the cube is spilt into two rectangular boxes, how much extra, in dollars, does it cost to paint the surfaces of the resulting two pieces?

47.

	/	/	
.	.	.	.
	0	0	0
1	1	1	1
2	2	2	2
3	3	3	3
4	4	4	4
5	5	5	5
6	6	6	6
7	7	7	7
8	8	8	8
9	9	9	9

48.

	/	/	
.	.	.	.
	0	0	0
1	1	1	1
2	2	2	2
3	3	3	3
4	4	4	4
5	5	5	5
6	6	6	6
7	7	7	7
8	8	8	8
9	9	9	9

Answer #47: $\frac{4}{3}$ or 1.33

Formula: • $\sqrt{\dfrac{a}{b}} = \dfrac{\sqrt{a}}{\sqrt{b}}$

Concepts: • Fractions
• Exponents and square roots

By taking the largest numerator from set N and the smallest denominator from set D, you get the largest possible fraction, $\frac{6}{3}$ = 2. Likewise, to generate the smallest possible fraction, take the smallest numerator from set N, 2, and the largest denominator from set D, 9, to get $\frac{2}{9}$.

The problem asks for the square root of the difference between the two fractions. The difference between 2 and $\frac{2}{9}$ is $2 - \frac{2}{9} = \frac{18}{9} - \frac{2}{9} = \frac{16}{9}$. The square root of $\frac{16}{9}$ can be computed as follows:

$$\sqrt{\frac{16}{9}} = \frac{\sqrt{16}}{\sqrt{9}} = \pm\frac{4}{3}.$$

Since you're asked for the *positive* square root, pick $\frac{4}{3}$.*

Answer #48:   6

Formula: • A cube has six faces
Concepts: • Rectangle geometry
• Diagramming

Because a cube has six faces and it costs $18 to paint the cube, it must cost $3 to paint each face. When you split the cube into two rectangular boxes, you create two new faces. At $3 per face, the additional cost of paint is $6.*

If you're having a hard time visualizing this problem the following illustration may help.

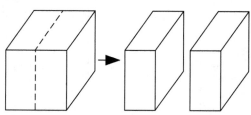

---

* Gridded-in answers to these problems appear on page 138.

49. A family consists of a pair of twin girls, age 6; a boy, age 10; and two parents, ages 38 and 40. What is the sum of the mean, the mode, and the median of their ages?

50.

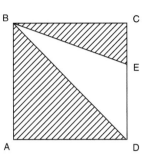

In this figure, ABCD is a square with area 2. If $\overline{DE}$ is twice as long as $\overline{EC}$, what is the area of $\triangle BED$?

49.

		/	/	
	.	.	.	.
		0	0	0
1	1	1	1	
2	2	2	2	
3	3	3	3	
4	4	4	4	
5	5	5	5	
6	6	6	6	
7	7	7	7	
8	8	8	8	
9	9	9	9	

50.

		/	/	
	.	.	.	.
		0	0	0
1	1	1	1	
2	2	2	2	
3	3	3	3	
4	4	4	4	
5	5	5	5	
6	6	6	6	
7	7	7	7	
8	8	8	8	
9	9	9	9	

Answer #49: 36

Definitions:
- Mean: This is another word for "average," this is the sum of the elements in a list divided by the number of elements in that list
- Mode: The element of a list that occurs most often
- Median: The element in a list for which half of the other elements are greater and the other half of the elements are less.

Concept:
- Averages

This problem is like a vocabulary quiz: if you know the definitions, you get the problem correct. The list of the family's ages, in ascending order, is {6, 6, 10, 38, 40}. The mode is the element that occurs the most often, 6. The median is the element in the middle. There are two ages greater than 10 and two less than 10, so 10 is the median. The mean is the sum of the ages divided by the number of ages. This comes out to:

$$\frac{6 + 6 + 10 + 38 + 40}{5} = \frac{100}{5} = 20.$$

So the sum of the mean, the mode, and the median of the family's ages is 6 + 10 + 20 = 36.*

Answer #50: $\frac{2}{3}$ or .666 or .667

Formulas:
- Area of triangle $= \frac{1}{2}$ x base × height
- Area of a square = length of a side squared

Concepts:
- Triangle geometry
- Rectangle geometry
- Diagramming

This problem states that ABCD has area 2. $\overline{BD}$ splits ABCD into 2 equal pieces, so $\triangle BCD$ has area 1. You are told that $\overline{ED}$ is twice as long as $\overline{CE}$, so add a point X that bisects $\overline{ED}$. Now you're left with three triangles: $\triangle BCE$, $\triangle BEX$, and $\triangle BXD$.

Because of where you chose to place X, the lengths of their bases are equal. Furthermore, they all share the altitude BC. So their areas must all be equal. Three equal triangles whose areas sum to 1 each have an area of $\frac{1}{3}$. The unshaded section of the square covers two of these triangles, so its area must be $\frac{2}{3}$.*

---

* Gridded-in answers to these problems appear on page 138.

SECTION 4

This final section of Test 1 consists of ten problems, each of which has five possible answer choices. For each problem, select the answer choice that represents the best solution and shade the corresponding oval.

---

51. All of the following pairs (x, y) satisfy the inequality $y \leq x^2$ *except*:

(A) $(1, -2)$
(B) $(2, 4)$
(C) $(-2, 4)$
(D) $(-3, 4)$
(E) $(-1, 2)$

52. If $(3^2)(2^3) = 2(6^m)$, then $m =$

(A) 1
(B) 2
(C) 3
(D) 4
(E) 5

---

51. (A) (B) (C) (D) (E)

52. (A) (B) (C) (D) (E)

Answer #51: Ⓔ

Concept: • Arithmetic

There are no complicated skills being tested in this problem, just your ability to keep a lot of numbers organized. The correct solution is E, because −1 squared is 1 and 1 < 2. All of the other options satisfy the relation $y \le x^2$.

   If you got this problem wrong, was it because you were working too fast? If so, slow down and pace yourself.

Answer #52: Ⓑ

Formula: • $a^n b^n = (ab)^n$
Concept: • Exponents

This is another problem that will take a relatively long time if you try to solve it by computing the values of all of the expressions but will go fairly quickly if you understand what's being tested. Instead of looking at the left side of the equation and immediately computing its value, step back and look for patterns.

   There's a 2 on the right side of the equation, so first factor a 2 out of the left side to get: $(3^2)(2^2)2 = 2(6^m)$. Now you can divide both sides of the equation by 2, leaving you with $(3^2)(2^2) = 6^m$. Using the formula shown above, you can further simplify the left side of the equation to be $(3 \times 2)^2$ and rewrite the equation as $6^2 = 6^m$. Having done only minimal multiplication, you can arrive at the answer, $m = 2$.

53.

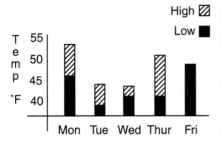

High and Low Temperatures for the Week

On which day of the week was the difference between the low and high temperatures the greatest?

(A) Monday
(B) Tuesday
(C) Wednesday
(D) Thursday
(E) Friday

54.

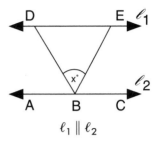

$\ell_1 \parallel \ell_2$

In the figure above, $\overline{BD}$ bisects $\angle ABE$ and $\overline{BE}$ bisects $\angle CBD$. What is the value of x?

(A) 30
(B) 45
(C) 60
(D) 90
(E) 120

53. (A) (B) (C) (D) (E)

54. (A) (B) (C) (D) (E)

Answer #53:   Ⓓ

Concept: • Tables and graphs

The low temperature for each day is represented by the dark bar in the chart. For example, on Monday, the low temperature was somewhere between 45 and 50 degrees. The high temperature for each day is represented by the light colored bar that sits on top of the darker bar—the graph designer could do this because she is guaranteed that the high temperature is always greater than or equal to the low temperature. On Monday the high temperature is almost 55 degrees. On Friday the high temperature and the low temperature are the same.

The difference between the high and low temperatures is the extra height added to each bar by the light colored section. By inspection, the bar with the largest light section is for Thursday, so the answer is D.

If you were unsure whether the answer is Monday or Thursday, note that on Monday the light bar is less than the difference between 45 and 55—that is, less than 10. The light bar on Thursday is slightly greater than the difference between 45 and 55, that is, more than 10.

Answer #54:   Ⓒ

Concepts: • Triangle geometry
   • Diagramming

When you're done working this problem, there should be three x's on the figure: the one originally there and two that you drew in. If you are going to perform well on the SAT, you *must* feel comfortable using and adding to the provided figures.

In this problem you're told that $\overline{BD}$ bisects $\angle ABE$. This means that the angles $\angle ABD$ and $\angle DBE$ have the same measure, $x°$. Similarly, because $\overline{BE}$ bisects $\angle CBD$, you can go through the same process and infer that $\angle CBE$ also has a measure of $x°$. Write these in.

Your diagram should now show a straight angle ($\angle ABC$) split into three equal parts. A straight angle has a measure of 180°, so each part must be 60°.

55. In a game of luck, there is a 1 in 10 chance of winning $10, a 1 in 5 chance of winning $5, and a 1 in 2 chance of winning $2. No other prizes are awarded, and a person cannot win more than one prize. What is the probability that a player will *not* win any money?

(A) 0
(B) .1
(C) .2
(D) .3
(E) 1

56.

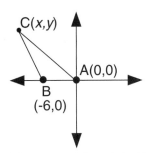

If the area of $\triangle ABC$ is 12, then the y-coordinate of C is:

(A) −4
(B) 4
(C) −2
(D) 2
(E) Cannot be determined from the information given

55. (A) (B) (C) (D) (E)

56. (A) (B) (C) (D) (E)

Answer #55: Ⓒ

Theorems:
- The probability that *either* of two independent, **exclusive** events will occur is the *sum* of their individual probabilities.
- The probability that *both* of two independent events will occur is the *product* of their individual probabilities.

Concepts:
- Probability
- Fractions

Probabilities, like ratios, decimals, and rates, involve computations with fractions.

The likelihood of a player winning a prize is either 1 in 10, 1 in 5, or 1 in 2. Written as fractions, these are $\frac{1}{10}, \frac{1}{5}$, and $\frac{1}{2}$. The probability that the player will win at least one of the prizes is the sum of the fractions:

$$\frac{1}{10} + \frac{1}{5} + \frac{1}{2} = \frac{8}{10} = \frac{4}{5}.$$

The probability that the player won't win any prize is the difference between 1 and the probability that the player will win a prize: $1 - \frac{4}{5} = \frac{1}{5}$.

Writing $\frac{1}{5}$ as a decimal yields .2, answer C.

Answer #56: Ⓑ

Formula:
- Area of a triangle $= \frac{1}{2} \times bh$

Concept:
- Coordinate geometry

You are given the area of △ABC, so it's likely you'll need to use the formula for the area of a triangle to find the *y*-coordinate of C, which is also the height of the perpendicular line segment from C down to the *x*-axis. Draw this in. Notice that this is an altitude of △ABC. Since the base of the triangle is 6, the length of $\overline{AB}$, you can plug into the formula:

$$\text{Area of } \triangle ABC = \frac{1}{2} \times \text{base} \times \text{height}$$

$$12 = \frac{1}{2} \times (6) \times (y)$$

$$4 = y$$

57. After the first two of four equal-length exams, Brenda had an 87% average. What is the lowest score Brenda can have on the third exam and still maintain at least a 90% average on all four tests?

(A) 83
(B) 86
(C) 87
(D) 93
(E) 96

58. A rhombus (a four-sided figure, all of whose sides are equal in length) has perimeter 20. If one of the diagonals has length 8, what is the length of the other diagonal?

(A) 3
(B) 5
(C) $5\sqrt{2}$
(D) 6
(E) 8

57. Ⓐ Ⓑ ⓒ Ⓓ Ⓔ

58. Ⓐ Ⓑ ⓒ Ⓓ Ⓔ

Answer #57: Ⓑ

Formula: • Average = $\dfrac{\text{sum of elements in a list}}{\text{number of elements in the list}}$

Concept: • Averages

Brenda received an average of 87% for the first two exams, so start by writing down: E_1: 87, E_2: 87. The problem is to find Brenda's score on the third exam, so write down E_3: x. Brenda wants to know how low she can score on the third exam and still be able to have a 90% average for the year; so, assume that she does the best she possibly can on the fourth exam, 100%. Now write down E_4: 100%.

Plugging into the equation for computing an average:

$$90 = \frac{87 + 87 + x + 100}{4}$$

Solving for x step by step, you write:

$$90 = \frac{274 + x}{4}$$

$$360 = 274 + x$$

$$86 = x$$

If Brenda wants to average at least 90% on the four tests, she must get at least 86% on the third exam. If she gets less than 86% on this exam, there's nothing she can do on the final exam to get a 90% overall average.

Answer #58: Ⓓ

Formulas: • Pythagorean theorem: $x^2 + y^2 = z^2$
    • A common "Pythagorean triple" is: $3^2 + 4^2 = 5^2$

Concepts: • Triangle geometry
    • Diagramming

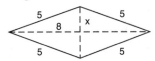

Start by drawing a picture. The figure has four equal sides. You know each side has a length of 5 because the perimeter is 20. The diagonal with the known length is marked with an 8; the other, unknown one with an x.

Notice that the two diagonals bisect each other and form a 90° angle. Knowing this, add two 4s to your picture in place of the 8 and mark the angle between the diagonals as 90°. Taking a look at any one of the four triangles formed by the diagonals, you have a hypotenuse of 5 and a side of 4 in a right triangle. This is a Pythagorean triple! You should recognize that the unknown side is 3. The unknown side of the triangle is half of the diagonal you are looking for, so the length of the diagonal is 6, answer D.

59. What is the smallest number greater than 1 that has both an integer square root and an integer cube root?

(A) 8
(B) 16
(C) 27
(D) 64
(E) 81

60. Two buses travel the same route. The first goes 55 miles per hour, the second goes 65 mph. How much farther has the faster bus driven after $3\frac{1}{2}$ hours?

(A) 10 miles
(B) 35 miles
(C) 192.5 miles
(D) 227.5 minutes
(E) 300 miles

59. Ⓐ Ⓑ Ⓒ Ⓓ Ⓔ

60. Ⓐ Ⓑ Ⓒ Ⓓ Ⓔ

Answer #59: Ⓓ

Formulas:
- $2^0 = 1, 2^1 = 2, 2^2 = 4, \ldots 2^6 = 64$
- $1^2 = 1, 2^2 = 4, 3^2 = 9, \ldots 9^2 = 81$
- $1^3 = 1, 2^3 = 8, 3^3 = 27, 4^3 = 64$

Concepts:
- Exponents
- Factoring and prime factors

Exponents get very big, very quickly. Consequently, to test your knowledge of exponents, the SAT has to use small exponents or small bases. Because of this, it is worth your time to memorize the powers of 2 up to 2^6 and the perfect squares and cubes less than 100.

This problem asks you to find the smallest number, call it x, that has both a square root and a cube root. Going through the list of possible solutions:

8 is a perfect cube but not a square
16 is a perfect square but not a cube
27 is a perfect cube but not a square
64 is both a perfect square and a perfect cube
81 is a perfect square but not a cube

64 is the only possibility that is both a perfect square and a perfect cube, so the answer is D.

Answer #60: Ⓑ

Formula:
- $\text{Rate} = \dfrac{\text{Amount}}{\text{Time}}$

Concept:
- Rates

I wanted to start this problem, "Two trains start in Chicago . . . ," but train problems are too clichéd for the SAT.

The simplest way to do this problem is to notice that the fast bus is going 10 mph faster than the slower bus. After $3\frac{1}{2}$ hours the faster bus has gone $3\frac{1}{2}$ hrs × 10 mph = 35 miles farther than the slow bus.

Another equally correct method of doing this problem is to figure out how far each bus went in $3\frac{1}{2}$ hours and then compute the difference. You should use the approach that takes you the least time and leaves you less prone to error.

Congratulations! You've now completed Test 1.

TEST 2

SECTION 1

This first section of Test 2 consists of 20 problems, each of which has five possible answer choices. For each problem, select the answer choice that represents the best solution and shade the corresponding oval.

1. If $1 + 2 + 3 + 4 + 5 + 6 = x + 7 + 11$, then $x =$

    (A) 1
    (B) 2
    (C) 3
    (D) 4
    (E) 5

2.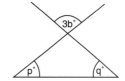

   From the diagram above, the sum of p and q, in terms of b, is:

    (A) $2b$
    (B) $3b$
    (C) $180 - b$
    (D) $180 - 2b$
    (E) $180 - 3b$

1. (A) (B) (C) (D) (E)

2. (A) (B) (C) (D) (E)

71

Answer #1:   Ⓒ

Concept: • Arithmetic

One of the goals of the SAT is to test your ability to avoid errors while problem solving. In this case you could do a lot of addition and simplify the equation to be: $21 = x + 18$. Working from there you would solve the equation and find that x is 3.

But there's a simpler route that involves fewer steps and is therefore less prone to error. Notice that $3 + 4 = 7$ and $5 + 6 = 11$. Consequently, you can subtract equal quantities from both sides of the equation, reducing it to $1 + 2 = x$. From here, the chances of you making an error are pretty slim!

Answer #2:   Ⓔ

Formulas: • Vertical angles have equal measures
                 • The sum of a triangle's angle measures is $180°$

Concept: • Triangle geometry

This problem asks you to find the "sum of p and q," $p + q$. Both p and q are angles of a triangle, so you can set up the equation $p + q + x = 180$, where x is the unknown angle at the top of the triangle. Because x and the angle with measure $3b°$ are vertical angles, they are equal and you can substitute $3b$ into your equation to get: $p + q + 3b = 180$. Now, subtract $3b$ from both sides of the equation, leaving $p + q = 180 - 3b$, answer E.

I. If $\dfrac{n}{2}$ is an even integer, then $\dfrac{n}{4}$ is an even integer.

II. If $\dfrac{n}{4}$ is an even integer, then $\dfrac{n}{2}$ is an even integer.

III. If $\dfrac{n}{4}$ is an odd integer, then $\dfrac{n}{2}$ is an even integer.

3. Which of the above statements is (are) true?

(A) I only
(B) II only
(C) I and II only
(D) I and III only
(E) II and III only

$$a = \frac{1}{x}$$

$$b = 9a$$

$$c = \frac{1}{b}$$

$$d = 9c$$

$$e = \frac{1}{d}$$

4. Given the above equations, $x =$

(A) a
(B) b
(C) c
(D) d
(E) e

3. Ⓐ Ⓑ Ⓒ Ⓓ Ⓔ

4. Ⓐ Ⓑ Ⓒ Ⓓ Ⓔ

Answer #3:   Ⓔ

Definition: • An even integer can be written as *2m* where *m* is another integer; for example, 6 is even because 2 × 3 = 6.

Concept: • Counterexamples☆

Before starting any calculations, notice that $\dfrac{n}{2}$ is 2 times $\dfrac{n}{4}$. Given this, you can read Statement I as, "If a number is even, then half of it is even." This isn't true; 2 is even and half of it, 1, is odd. *Any time you can come up with a counterexample to a statement, it is definitely false;* however, finding an example of a statement does not necessarily make it true.

　　Statement II says, "If an integer is even, then twice the integer is even." The definition of an even number is a number that is twice *any* integer, so Statement II is clearly true. Likewise, Statement III considers only numbers that are twice odd numbers, so it, too, is true. Statement I is false, and Statements II and III are true, so the correct answer is E.

Answer #4:   Ⓓ

Theorem: • $\dfrac{1}{a/b} = b/a$

Concept: • Fractions

This problem requires, more than anything else, for you to be careful. You are told that $a = \dfrac{1}{x}$, so answer A, $x = a$, can't be correct. Now, in the second equation, plug $\dfrac{1}{x}$ in for *a*. You should get $b = 9\left(\dfrac{1}{x}\right) = \dfrac{9}{x}$. Proceed with the third equation: Plug $\dfrac{9}{x}$ in for *b* to get $c = \dfrac{1}{9/x} = \dfrac{x}{9}$. (Notice here that 1 over a fraction simply inverts the fraction.) Continue with the fourth equation by plugging in $\dfrac{x}{9}$ for *c* to get $d = 9\left(\dfrac{x}{9}\right) = x$. And there's your answer: $x = d$, answer D.

☆ See Concept-to-Problem Index page 141.

5. For positive x and y, $x^2 + 2xy + y^2 = 36$. What is the average of x and y?

(A) 3
(B) 6
(C) 12
(D) 18
(E) Cannot be determined from the information given

6.

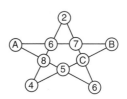

If the sums of the numbers along any line segment of the star are equal, then $B =$

(A) 3
(B) 4
(C) 5
(D) 6
(E) 7

5. Ⓐ Ⓑ Ⓒ Ⓓ Ⓔ

6. Ⓐ Ⓑ Ⓒ Ⓓ Ⓔ

Answer #5:   Ⓐ

Formula: • $x^2 + 2xy + y^2 = (x + y)^2$

Definition: • Average $= \dfrac{\text{sum of the items in a list}}{\text{number of items in the list}}$

Concepts: • Averages
• Polynomial arithmetic

Because you need to find the average of x and y, you should start looking for ways to find $x + y$ so you can compute their average. Knowing that you are looking for $x + y$ should remind you that $x^2 + 2xy + y^2$ can be written in the form $(x + y)^2$. Because $x^2 + 2xy + y^2 = 36$, it is also true that $(x + y)^2 = 36$. Taking the square root of both sides of the equation, you get $x + y = \pm 6$. Because x and y are defined to be positive, $x + y = 6$.

Now you can compute the average of x and y as $\dfrac{x + y}{2} = \dfrac{6}{2} = 3$, answer A.

Answer #6:   Ⓓ

Concept: • Arithmetic

Consider the problem statement, "The sums of the numbers along any line segment of the star are equal." This suggests that your first step is to find the sums.

Notice that the line between the lower left corner and the top consists of only numbers and no unknowns. Summing 4, 8, 6, and 2 you should get 20, so the sum of 4 numbers along any line of the star is 20.

You can't compute B yet because the two lines containing B also contain another unknown variable; one contains A and one C. Your next step can be to compute either A or C. To compute A, consider the line of numbers between the upper left and the lower right, A, 8, 5, and 6. You know that these add to 20, so you can write the equation $A + 8 + 5 + 6 = 20$. Solving this gives you $A = 1$. Replace the A in the diagram with a 1.

Now the line between the top left and top right of the star has B as its only variable, and from it you can set up the equation $1 + 6 + 7 + B = 20$. Solving for B, you should get 6, answer D.

7.

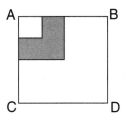

The three squares pictured above share a common vertex at A. The two interior squares each have a second vertex at the center of the next larger square. What is the ratio of the area of the shaded region to the area of the unshaded region?

(A) 3 : 4
(B) 3 : 8
(C) 3 : 12
(D) 3 : 13
(E) 3 : 16

8. For positive x, which of the following quantities is greatest?

(A) $\dfrac{1}{x}$

(B) $\sqrt{x}$

(C) x

(D) x^2

(E) Cannot be determined from the information given

7. Ⓐ Ⓑ Ⓒ Ⓓ Ⓔ

8. Ⓐ Ⓑ Ⓒ Ⓓ Ⓔ

Answer #7:   Ⓓ

Formula: • Area of a square = s^2

Concepts: • Rectangle geometry
              • Diagramming

By adding lines to the drawing, you should be able to figure the answer with little more effort than it takes to count. Here's the same figure as given in the problem:

You can add the lines as I've done here because the problem stated that each of the smaller squares has a vertex at the center of the next larger square. The dashed lines make it clear that three small boxes are gray and the remaining 13 are unshaded, so the ratio of gray to unshaded boxes is 3:13, answer D.

If you selected answer E, you probably were describing the fractional part of square ABCD that is gray. Confusing fractions and ratios is an easy mistake to make; don't get caught.

Answer #8:   Ⓔ

Concepts: • Fractions
              • Exponents and square roots

The values of x, $\frac{1}{x}$, $\sqrt{x}$, and x^2 behave somewhat counterintuitively with respect to each other when x is between −1 and 1. For example, x^2 is usually greater than x; however, when x is $\frac{1}{2}$, x^2 is $\frac{1}{4}$.

By plugging in first $x = \frac{1}{2}$ and then $x = 2$, you can show that none of the quantities listed in the solutions is always greater than the others, so the answer is E.

9. At a movie theater, the cost of an adult ticket is $7.50, and the cost of a student ticket is $3.75. If 500 people see a movie and spend a total of $2,250.00, how many of the people who saw the movie were students?

(A) 100
(B) 200
(C) 300
(D) 400
(E) Cannot be determined from the information given

10. What is the maximum number of 6 × 10 rectangles that can be placed in a 28 × 105 rectangle if the 6 × 10 rectangles must have the same orientation and may not overlap?

(A) 7
(B) 34
(C) 40
(D) 42
(E) 49

9. Ⓐ Ⓑ Ⓒ Ⓓ Ⓔ

10. Ⓐ Ⓑ Ⓒ Ⓓ Ⓔ

Answer #9:   Ⓓ

Concept: • Solving equations

Let the number of adults be A and the number of students be S. Your first equation describes the number of people who saw the movie: $A + S = 500$.

The second equation deals with the amount of money collected:

$$\frac{15}{2}A + \frac{15}{4}S = 2,250$$

Notice that I converted \$7.50 to $\frac{15}{2}$ dollars. For me, it is much easier to manipulate fractions than decimal points.

There are many ways to solve the two equations. One is to multiply both sides of the second equation by $\frac{4}{15}$ to get: $2A + S = 600$. Then you can subtract the first equation from the second as follows:

$$2A + S = 600$$
$$\underline{A + S = 500}$$
$$A \qquad = 100$$

Plugging in 100 for A into either of the original equations allows you to solve for S and find that $S = 400$, the number of students who saw the movie.

Answer #10:   Ⓒ

Concept: • Diagramming

Think of the big rectangle as having horizontal length 105 and width 28. You can place the 6 × 10 rectangles into the large one either horizontally or vertically. In the first case the width is 6, so you can fit four of these going down because 4 × 6 = 24, leaving four units at the bottom. The length is 10, so you can fit ten across, leaving five units at the end. In this case, the total number of small rectangles that fit inside the large one is 4 × 10 = 40.

If you're having a hard time visualizing this, draw a picture.

If you place the small rectangles vertically, you can fit only 2 down and 17 across, for a total of 2 × 17 = 34. Thus, the first orientation fits more rectangles, and the answer is C, 40.

11. How many integers between 10 and 100, inclusive, are perfect squares?

(A) 5
(B) 6
(C) 7
(D) 9
(E) 10

12. An $8'' \times 11''$ piece of paper is to be folded twice, parallel to its $8''$ edge, so that it fits into an $8''$ by $4''$ envelope. The folds divide the paper into three sections. What is the minimum possible area of a section if the letter is to fit into the envelope?

(A) 3 in^2
(B) 4 in^2
(C) 8 in^2
(D) 24 in^2
(E) 32 in^2

11. Ⓐ Ⓑ Ⓒ Ⓓ Ⓔ

12. Ⓐ Ⓑ Ⓒ Ⓓ Ⓔ

Answer #11: Ⓒ

Concept: • Exponents and square roots

One approach to this problem is to have memorized all of the perfect squares less than 100. Although you should be familiar with the perfect squares, the chance of you accidentally missing one using this method is too high to rely on memory alone.

Instead, notice that $16 = 4^2$ is the first perfect square after 10. And $100 = 10^2$ is itself a perfect square. Now you can say that the perfect squares between 10 and 100 are the same as the perfect squares between 4^2 and 10^2, which can be readily enumerated: $4^2, 5^2, \ldots, 9^2, 10^2$.

At this point, resort to your fingers and count: there are 7 integers from 4 to 10, answer C.

Answer #12: Ⓓ

Concept: • Given a fixed amount partitioned into groups, if one group is larger, the rest of the groups are smaller. ☆

This is a tough problem to visualize. It's extremely helpful to draw a picture of what's going on; or, better yet, if you have the scrap paper, try folding it as the problem describes.

To minimize the area of one of the three sections, you need to make the other two sections as large as possible. The longest any one section can be and still fit into the envelope is 4 inches. If two sections are 4 inches long, then the last section is 11 inches − 4 inches − 4 inches = 3 inches.

The area of a section that is 3 inches long and 8 inches wide is $3 \times 8 = 24$ square inches, answer D.

13. Of the two-digit numbers (i.e., those from 10 to 99, inclusive), how many have a second digit greater than the first digit?

(A) 36
(B) 40
(C) 41
(D) 45
(E) 50

14. A uniformly thick ribbon of whipped cream flows out of the circular opening of a whipped cream can at a uniform rate of $5 \frac{\text{cm}}{\text{second}}$. If the radius of the opening is halved, how much faster would the whipped cream have to flow to deliver the same *volume* of output in the same amount of time?

(A) $1x$
(B) $2x$
(C) $3x$
(D) $4x$
(E) $8x$

13. (A) (B) (C) (D) (E)

14. (A) (B) (C) (D) (E)

Answer #13: (A)
Concept: • Patterns☆

There are many ways of approaching this problem. One is to look at each possible first digit as a separate case. Of the two-digit numbers that begin with a 1, all except 10 and 11 have a second digit greater than the first. In this case, all is 12, 13, . . . 19—eight numbers. By the same reason, of the two-digit numbers that begin with a 2, all except the 20, 21, and 22 have a second digit greater than the first. In this case, all is 23, 24, . . . 29—seven numbers.

Have you spotted the pattern yet? Each time you increase the first digit by one, there's one less number that can be formed whose second digit is greater than the first. Consequently, the total number of two-digit numbers whose second digit is greater than the first is $8 + 7 + 6 \ldots + 1 = 36$.

Answer #14: (D)
Formulas: • Area of a circle = πr^2
                • Rate = $\dfrac{\text{Amount}}{\text{Time}}$
Concepts: • Rates
                • Circle geometry

Usually, rates are given in distance over time; however, a rate can be anything that changes over time. In this problem you're asked to consider both a linear rate, how fast the ribbon comes out of the can, and a volumetric rate or flow, how much whipped cream comes out of the can. To help differentiate between the two, contrast a very thin stream and a thick one. The thin stream can come out very quickly but won't amount to much while the thick stream can come out more slowly but will pile up quickly.

Let r be the original radius of the opening and s be the original linear speed of the cream. The area of the opening can be computed to be πr^2 and the flow rate can be computed to be $\pi r^2 s$.

Likewise, let $\dfrac{r}{2}$ be the final radius of the opening (you are told it is halved) and let S be the final linear speed of the whipped cream. By the same reasoning, the final flow rate can be computed to be $\dfrac{\pi r^2 S}{4}$.

You are told that the original and final flow rates are the same so you can write the equality:
$$\pi r^2 s = \frac{\pi r^2 S}{4}$$

Dividing out the common factors you are left with $s = \dfrac{S}{4}$ or $S = 4s$—the final speed is four times the original one, answer D.

15. Dan pays $250 to a broker who finds him an apartment for $500 a month. Heidi finds an apartment by herself for $550 a month. If Heidi and Dan start paying rent at the same time, and the broker's fee is paid in advance, after how many months will they have spent the same amount?

(A) 1
(B) 4
(C) 5
(D) 6
(E) 10

16. In a prehistoric village, rocks, stones, and pebbles were used for money. The relative values of the "coins" were:

1 rock = 7 stones

1 stone = 7 pebbles

If a person used 6 rocks to purchase a hide that cost 5 rocks, 2 stones, and 3 pebbles, how much would the change be?

(A) 1 rock, 5 stones, 4 pebbles
(B) 5 stones, 4 pebbles
(C) 4 stones, 4 pebbles
(D) 5 stones, 5 pebbles
(E) 6 stones, 5 pebbles

15. Ⓐ Ⓑ Ⓒ Ⓓ Ⓔ

16. Ⓐ Ⓑ Ⓒ Ⓓ Ⓔ

Answer #15: Ⓒ

Concept: • Word problems

Each month Heidi pays $50 more than Dan. Restated, the problem asks how many months will pass before the amount that Dan saves by having a lesser rent equals his broker's fee of $250. To compute this, divide the $250 broker's fee by $50 to get $\dfrac{250}{50} = \dfrac{25}{5} = 5$.

Answer #16: Ⓒ

Concept: • Solving equations

One way of attacking this problem would be to subtract 5 rocks, 2 stones, and 3 pebbles from 6 rocks; however, subtraction on rocks isn't something that many people are practiced at! Instead, try inverting the subtraction problem: ask the question, "How much do I have to add to 5 rocks, 2 stones, and 3 pebbles to reach 6 rocks?"

To solve this question, first add 4 pebbles to 5 rocks, 2 stones, and 3 pebbles. This gives you 5 rocks, 2 stones, and 7 pebbles. But, 7 pebbles is a stone, so you have 5 rocks and 3 stones.

Next add 4 stones to your 5 rocks and 3 stones. This gives you 5 rocks and 7 stones. But, 7 stones is a rock, so you have 6 rocks.

All together you needed to add 4 stones and 4 pebbles to make up for the difference between the cost of the hide and the amount paid. Therefore, the amount of change owed is answer C, 4 stones and 4 pebbles.

17. If the ratio of the altitude of triangle A to the altitude of triangle B is 2:1, then the ratio of the area of triangle A to the area of triangle B is:

(A) 1:1
(B) 2:1
(C) 3:1
(D) 4:1
(E) Cannot be determined from the information given

18. All of the following are equal to 368 *except*:

(A) 300 + 60 + 8
(B) 10(30 + 6) + 8
(C) 100(3) + 10(6) + 1(8)
(D) 10(30) + 68
(E) 300 + 10(6 + 8)

17. Ⓐ Ⓑ Ⓒ Ⓓ Ⓔ

18. Ⓐ Ⓑ Ⓒ Ⓓ Ⓔ

Answer #17: Ⓔ

Formula:
- Area of a triangle $= \frac{1}{2}bh$

Concept:
- Triangle geometry

Although you know the ratio of the altitude of ∆A to the altitude of ∆B, you know nothing about the relationship of their bases. Therefore, you have no way of determining the relationship of their areas.

Answer #18: Ⓔ

Concept:
- Arithmetic

Remember that multiplying a number by 10 is the same as adding a 0 onto the end of it (e.g., $8 \times 10 = 80$). You also know that $368 = 300 + 60 + 8$.

To solve this problem, you need to find the expression that adds the wrong number of zeroes to either the 3, 6, or 8. In answer E, the 8 is being multiplied by 10 to give you 80 instead of 8. Therefore, in answer E, $300 + 10(6 + 8) \neq 368$.

19.

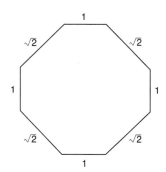

The sides of an octagon alternate in length, as pictured above. What is the area of the octagon?

(A) 5
(B) 6
(C) 7
(D) 8
(E) 9

Note: Question 20 refers to the following definition:

$$\begin{bmatrix} a & b \\ c & d \end{bmatrix} = \frac{1}{ad - bc}$$

20. Which of the following has a value that is not defined?

(A) $\begin{bmatrix} 1 & 2 \\ 3 & 4 \end{bmatrix}$

(B) $\begin{bmatrix} 2 & 3 \\ 5 & 7 \end{bmatrix}$

(C) $\begin{bmatrix} 4 & 3 \\ 8 & 6 \end{bmatrix}$

(D) $\begin{bmatrix} 2 & -2 \\ 4 & 4 \end{bmatrix}$

(E) $\begin{bmatrix} -3 & -2 \\ 6 & -4 \end{bmatrix}$

19. Ⓐ Ⓑ Ⓒ Ⓓ Ⓔ

20. Ⓐ Ⓑ Ⓒ Ⓓ Ⓔ

Answer #19: ©

Concepts: • Rectangle geometry
• Diagramming

If you add the following lines to the octagon and remember that the diagonal of a square is $\sqrt{2}$ times as long as its side, it should be clear that the octagon is really made up of five whole squares and four half-squares.

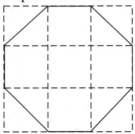

The total of five whole squares and four half-squares is seven squares. Each square has area $1 \times 1 = 1$ because the sides have length 1. Thus, the total area of the octagon is $7 \times 1 = 7$, answer C.

Answer #20: ©

Definition: • Division by 0 is not defined.
Concept: • Functions

Notice that $\begin{bmatrix} a & b \\ c & d \end{bmatrix}$ is defined to be the fraction $\dfrac{1}{ad - bc}$, so you need to find a fraction with an undefined value. You know that a fraction can never have a 0 in the denominator, so to find the expression without a value, you need to find the one where $ad - bc = 0$.

In solution:

(A), $ad - bc = (1)(4) - (2)(3) = 4 - 6 = -2$

(B), $ad - bc = (2)(7) - (3)(5) = 14 - 15 = -1$

(C), $ad - bc = (4)(6) - (3)(8) = 24 - 24 = 0$

The correct answer is answer C because

$\begin{bmatrix} 4 & 3 \\ 8 & 6 \end{bmatrix} = \dfrac{1}{(4)(6) - (3)(8)} = \dfrac{1}{0}$, which has an undefined value.

SECTION 2

Questions 21–35 each consist of two quantities, one in Column A and one in Column B. You are to compare the two quantities and on the answer sheet fill in:

A   if the quantity in Column A is greater
B   if the quantity in Column B is greater
C   if the two quantities are equal
D   if the relationship cannot be determined from the information given

AN E RESPONSE WILL NOT BE SCORED

NOTES:

1. In certain questions, information concerning one or both of the quantities to be compared is centered above the two columns.
2. In a given question, a symbol that appears in both columns represents the same thing in Column A as it does in Column B.
3. Letters such as x, n, and k stand for real numbers.

EXAMPLES		
	Column A	Column B
E1.	2×6	$2 + 6$
E2.	$180 - x$	y
E3.	$p - q$	$q - p$

E2 figure: a horizontal line with a ray extending upward to the right, forming angles $x°$ and $y°$.

E1. ● Ⓑ Ⓒ Ⓓ
E2. Ⓐ Ⓑ ● Ⓓ
E3. Ⓐ Ⓑ Ⓒ ●

21.

$$[a,b,c] = \frac{abc}{3}$$

Column A	Column B
[3,3,3]	The average of 3, 3, and 3

22.

$$x < y$$

Column A	Column B
$(x - y)^2$	$(y - x)^2$

21. Ⓐ Ⓑ Ⓒ Ⓓ

22. Ⓐ Ⓑ Ⓒ Ⓓ

Answer #21: (A)

Definition: • Average = $\dfrac{\text{sum of the items in a list}}{\text{number of items in the list}}$

Concepts: • Averages
• Functions

Column A consists of [3,3,3], which is defined to be $\dfrac{3 \times 3 \times 3}{3}$. A 3 in the numerator and the 3 in the denominator cancel one another out, and you are left with $3 \times 3 = 9$.

Column B is the average of three 3's. You can calculate the average to be $\dfrac{3+3+3}{3} = 3$. You could also have noticed that the average of any number of 3's is always 3, saving yourself some arithmetic.

Since $9 > 3$, the answer is A.

Answer #22: (C)

Formulas: • $(a - b) = -1(b - a)$
• $x^2 = (-x)^2$ for all x

Concept: • Exponents and square roots

Notice that $(x - y)$ and $(y - x)$ are negatives of one another. For example, $5 - 2 = 3$ and $2 - 5 = -3$. Knowing this, you can deduce that these squares are equal. Hence, Columns A and B are equal, answer C.

If you didn't remember that $(x - y) = (-1)(y - x)$, you could have multiplied out $(x - y)^2$ and $(y - x)^2$ and compared the terms.

Note that the $x < y$ given in the problem statement was superfluous (a good word for the vocabulary section of the SAT!).

23.

$$0 < a < x$$
$$0 < b < y$$

Column A	Column B
$\dfrac{x + a}{y - b}$	$\dfrac{x - a}{y + b}$

24.

A truck must make three deliveries. The first is one mile from the store. The second is one mile from the first delivery. The third is one mile from the second delivery.

Column A	Column B
The distance from the third delivery to the store	The distance from the first delivery to the third

23. Ⓐ Ⓑ Ⓒ Ⓓ

24. Ⓐ Ⓑ Ⓒ Ⓓ

Answer #23: Ⓐ

Theorems:
- Given two fractions with equal denominators, the one with the larger numerator is larger.
- Given two fractions with equal numerators, the one with the larger denominator is smaller.

Concept:
- Fractions

Start with the fraction $\dfrac{x}{y}$. In Column A, the numerator is increased and the denominator is decreased. Both of these operations increase the value of the fraction, so you can write $\dfrac{x+a}{y-b} > \dfrac{x}{y}$.

Likewise, in Column B the numerator is less than x, and the denominator is greater than y. Both of these operations decrease the value of the fraction, so $\dfrac{x-a}{y+b} < \dfrac{x}{y}$.

Putting these together: $\dfrac{x+a}{y-b} > \dfrac{x}{y} > \dfrac{x-a}{y+b}$. The value in Column A is greater than the value in Column B, answer A.

Answer #24: Ⓓ

Concepts:
- Nonlinearity☆
- Diagramming

People often limit their thinking to a line. For example, you could draw the truck's delivery route as follows:

This is NOT the only possible configuration, however. Another possible delivery route is:

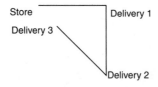

In fact, there are infinite ways to draw the delivery map from the information stated in the problem. In short, you can't compute the distances between the first and third delivery or between the third delivery and the store, so the correct answer is D.

☆ See Concept-to-Problem Index page 141.

25. $ab < 0$

$ac > 0$

Column A	Column B
0	bc

26. As Lauren was going to math class, she met a man with 12 wives. Each wife carried 10 sacks, each sack contained 4 cats. While returning home, Lauren met a woman with 16 husbands. Each husband carried 6 sacks, each sack contained 5 dogs.

Column A	Column B
The number of cats Lauren encountered while going to math class	The number of dogs Lauren encountered while returning home

25. Ⓐ Ⓑ Ⓒ Ⓓ

26. Ⓐ Ⓑ Ⓒ Ⓓ

Answer #25: Ⓐ

Theorems: • Negative × negative = positive
              • Negative × positive = negative
              • Positive × positive = positive

Concepts: • Inequalities
              • Arithmetic

You are being asked to compare bc with 0. If bc is negative, then Column A is greater; if bc is 0, then the two columns are equal; and if bc is positive, then Column B is greater.

Because $ab < 0$ you know that a and b have different signs—that is, one is negative and the other is positive. Because $ac > 0$, you know that a and c have the same sign: either both are positive or both are negative. Combining these two facts, you can conclude that b and c have different signs. Therefore, $bc < 0$, and Column A is greater than Column B.

Another approach is to multiply both sides of $ab < 0$ by ac. This yields $a^2bc < 0$. a can't be zero because $ab \neq 0$; so a^2 must be positive. Therefore, you can divide both sides of the inequality by a^2 to get $bc < 0$, what is in Column B is less than what is in Column A.

Answer #26: Ⓒ

Concept: • Arithmetic

On her way to math class, Lauren met 12 wives, each of whom was carrying 10 sacks. This is a total of 12 × 10 = 120 sacks. Each sack contained 4 cats, for a total of 120 × 4 = 480 cats.

On her way home, Lauren met 16 husbands, each of whom was carrying 6 sacks. This is a total of 16 × 6 = 96 sacks. Each sack contained 5 dogs, for a total of 96 × 5 = 480 dogs.

The number of cats and dogs is the same, so the answer is C.

Questions 27 and 28 refer to the following graph:

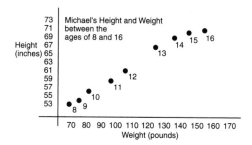

27.

Column A	Column B
Age at which Michael's height changed the fastest	Age at which Michael's weight changed the fastest

28.

Column A	Column B
Age at which Michael's weight increased the fastest with respect to his height	13

27. Ⓐ Ⓑ Ⓒ Ⓓ

28. Ⓐ Ⓑ Ⓒ Ⓓ

Answer #27: Ⓒ

Concept: • Tables and graphs

Michael's height is the *y*-coordinate of each point representing his age, and his weight is the *x*-coordinate. For example, at age 9, Michael was approximately 54 inches tall.

The change in Michael's height from one year to the next is the vertical distance between successive points in the graph. For example, from age 8 to 9 Michael's height went from 53 to 54 inches, increasing approximately 1 inch. By looking at the graph, you should be able to see that the largest change in height from one year to the next occurs from age 12 to 13, when he grows approximately 6 inches. Hence, Michael's height changed the fastest at age 12.

Using the same logic, the largest horizontal distance (i.e., change in his weight) between two successive years occurred during the same period. Notice that you never need to compute the actual values of the height and weight changes. All you need to know is that between the ages of 12 and 13 both Michael's height and weight were changing the fastest of any time on the graph.

Answer #28: Ⓐ

Concept: • Tables and graphs

Between the ages of 8 and 15, Michael tended to gain approximately $4\frac{1}{2}$ pounds for each inch he grew. This is approximately constant because the points representing his height and weight from age 8 to 15 all fall on a line. Between 15 and 16, however, Michael grows only slightly taller but puts on a lot more weight. Consequently, between ages 15 and 16 his weight changed fastest with respect to his height.

29.

In January the average amount spent per person at a grocery store was $63. In February the average rose to $69 per person.

Column A	Column B
The average amount spent per person during the two months	$66

30.

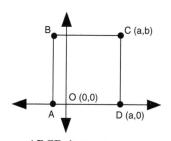

ABCD is a square
C is the point with coordinates (a,b)
D is the point with coordinates $(a,0)$
O is the origin

Column A	Column B
a	b

29. Ⓐ Ⓑ Ⓒ Ⓓ

30. Ⓐ Ⓑ Ⓒ Ⓓ

Answer #29:   Ⓓ

Definition: • Average $= \dfrac{\text{sum of the items in a list}}{\text{number of items in the list}}$

Concept: • Averages

It isn't possible to take two averages and combine them to generate a third. The reasoning is best shown by example. In this problem, consider the extreme situation where only one person shopped at the store in January and spent $63, but during February 999 people shopped at the store and spent $69 each. The average amount spent by the one person during January is $63. The average amount spent by the 999 people during February is $69. However, it's definitely not the case that over the two months the 1,000 people spent an average of $66. In this hypothetical situation the average over the two months is much closer to $69. You can also create a situation where a lot of people spend $63 in January and very few people spend $69 in February, thereby bringing the average down.

Given these two hypothetical situations, you know that the average amount spent per person at the store during the two months is not necessarily greater than or less than $66, so the answer is D.

Answer #30:   Ⓑ

Concepts: • Coordinate geometry
          • Rectangle geometry

The length of $\overline{DC}$ is the distance from $(a,0)$ to (a,b), which is b. Add this information to the diagram. ABCD is a square, so its four sides all have the same length, b—add this, too, to the diagram. The length of $\overline{OD}$, from $(0,0)$ to $(a,0)$, is a. Add this information to the diagram.

Now step back and look at what you have. $\overline{AD}$ has length b and $\overline{OD}$ has length a, so b is clearly greater than a.

31.

$n > 0$

Column A	Column B
The sum of n numbers divided by the average of the n numbers	n

32.

Two equivalent circles are drawn inside a third circle in such a way that they each are tangent to the third circle and share a single common point at the center of the circle.

Column A	Column B
The shaded area	The area of one of the small circles

31. Ⓐ Ⓑ Ⓒ Ⓓ

32. Ⓐ Ⓑ Ⓒ Ⓓ

Answer #31: Ⓒ

Definition: • The average of n numbers is the sum of the numbers divided by n.

Concepts: • Averages
   • Fractions

Let the sum of the n numbers be S. Then, by definition, their average is $\frac{S}{n}$. Column A isn't the average of the numbers; rather, it's the sum divided by the average. You write this $\dfrac{S}{\left(\frac{S}{n}\right)}$. Simplifying this expression you get: $\dfrac{S}{\left(\frac{S}{n}\right)} = S \times \dfrac{n}{S} = n$. This is exactly what is in column B, so the values in the two columns are equal and the correct answer is C.

Answer #32: Ⓒ

Definition: • Area of circle = πr^2

Concept: • Circle geometry

Let the radius of the small circles be r (draw it in the illustration). It follows that the area of each small circle is πr^2. That's the value of Column B.

The shaded region is shaped oddly enough that you're not going to be able to find a neat formula for computing its area. Instead, compute the area of the large circle. The radius of the large circle is the same as the diameter of the small circles, $2r$, so its area is $\pi(2r)^2 = 4\pi r^2$. Subtracting the 2 smaller circles from the large circle, you're left with $4\pi r^2 - 2(\pi r^2) = 2\pi r^2$. This is the area of both the top and bottom oddly shaped regions. Divide this by 2 and you get the area of the shaded region, $\frac{1}{2}2\pi r^2 = \pi r^2$, which is the same as the area of a smaller circle, so the answer is C.

33. On a form, dates are encoded as six-digit integers. The first two digits represent the last two digits of the year (e.g., 93 for 1993), the second two digits represent the month (01 for January, 02 for February, . . .), and the third two digits are the day of the month.

Column A	Column B
The encoding of February 12, 1964	The encoding of November 06, 2009

34.

Column A	Column B
The length of the third side of a right triangle having two sides of length 1 and $\sqrt{2}$	$\sqrt{3}$

33. Ⓐ Ⓑ Ⓒ Ⓓ

34. Ⓐ Ⓑ Ⓒ Ⓓ

Answer #33: Ⓐ

Concept: • Following directions☆

The encoding of February 12, 1964, is 640212. The first two digits, 64, are the last two digits of the year. The second two digits of the encoding, 02, are the month. And, the last two digits, 12, are the day.

Likewise, the encoding of November 06, 2009, is 091106. 09 for the year, 11 for the month, and 06 for the day.

Dropping the leading zero and adding commas to make the numbers more readable, the value in Column A is 640,212, and the value in Column B is 91,106. Column A is clearly greater.

Answer #34: Ⓓ

Definition: • In a right triangle, $c^2 = a^2 + b^2$, where c is the length of the side opposite the right angle, and a and b are the lengths of the legs.

Concept: • Triangle geometry

There are three possible right triangles with sides 1 and $\sqrt{2}$. The hypotenuse can be either the side of unknown length, the side with length 1, or the side with length $\sqrt{2}$. In fact, the side with length 1 can't be the hypotenuse because the hypotenuse of a right triangle is always the longest side, and $1 < \sqrt{2}$ so you are left with the following two possibilities:

In the first case, the unknown side is the hypotenuse, so you can set up the equation $x^2 = 1^2 + (\sqrt{2})^2 = 3$. Solving this for x, you get $x = \sqrt{3}$.

In the second case, the side with length $\sqrt{2}$ is the hypotenuse, so you can set up the equation: $x^2 = (\sqrt{2})^2 - 1^2 = 1$. Solving this for x, you get $x = 1$.

In the first case, the value in Column A equals the value in Column B, and, in the second case, the value in Column A is less than that in Column B, so their relationship is indeterminate, answer D.

35.

$$b \neq 0$$
$$b^2 - 4ac < 0$$
$$a < 0$$

Column A	Column B
c	0

---

35. Ⓐ Ⓑ Ⓒ Ⓓ

Answer #35: Ⓑ

Theorems:
- Negative × negative = positive
- Negative × positive = negative
- Positive × negative = negative
- Positive × positive = positive
- The same rules hold for division as well

Concept:
- Inequalities

Start with the expression that was given in the problem statement, $b^2 - 4ac < 0$, and add $4ac$ to both sides of the inequality to get: $b^2 < 4ac$. You know that b^2 can't be negative, so $4ac$ must be a positive number. Dividing a positive number by 4 yields another positive number, so you know that ac must be positive. The only way ac can be positive is if both a and c have the same sign. You are told that a is negative, so c must also be negative. Any negative number is less than 0, so the value in Column A is less than the value in Column B.

SECTION 3

This section of the test requires you to enter your solution to each of the following fifteen problems onto a grid. The grid consists of four columns and twelve rows. To enter a number onto the grid, write each of the digits, in order, into the boxes at the top of the grid. Then shade in the corresponding box beneath the digit. A decimal point is provided for numbers such as .5, and a slash is provided for constructing fractions such as $\frac{1}{2}$. The following are examples of correctly entered numbers:

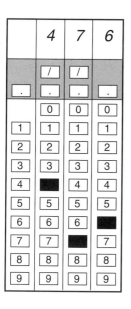
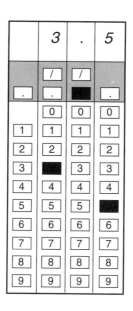
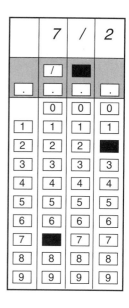

Remember the following when entering numbers onto the grid:

- Mark no more than one space in any column.

- No question will have a negative answer.

- If your answer is a *fraction*, remember to grid-in the fraction line in its own column.

- If your answer contains a *decimal point,* you must enter it in its own column.

- *Mixed numbers*, such as $3\frac{1}{2}$, must be gridded-in using decimals (i.e., 3.5) or as improper fractions (i.e., 7/2). If you enter your answer as a mixed number, it will be incorrect. In the case of $3\frac{1}{2}$, for example, the machine scoring your test will interpret $3\frac{1}{2}$ as $\frac{31}{2} = 15.5$.

If the answer to a problem is a repeating decimal, such as .3333 . . . (or $.\overline{3}$), round your solution to the most accurate answer the grid can accommodate (i.e., .333). Less accurate values, such as .3, will be considered incorrect.

36. If $w \neq 0$, $x = \dfrac{1}{2}y$, and $w = 2x$, then $\dfrac{y}{w} =$

37. When a 100-seat movie theater sells tickets for $6 apiece, it can fill 35 of the seats. When tickets cost $5 apiece, the theater can sell 50 tickets. In dollars, how much greater are the ticket sales when the theater sells tickets at the $5 price than at the $6 price?

Answer #36: 1
Concept: • Fractions

You are told that $w = 2x$ and $x = \dfrac{1}{2}y$, and you're being asked to find $\dfrac{y}{w}$. This suggests that you want to find expressions for both y and w in terms of x. To start, the equation $w = 2x$ already states w in terms of x. Multiplying both sides of the equation $x = \dfrac{1}{2}y$ by 2, you get $2x = y$. Now substitute into $\dfrac{y}{w}$ to get $\dfrac{2x}{2x}$ or, more simply put, 1.*

Answer #37: 40
Concept: • Word problems

At the $5 price, the theater sells 50 tickets for a gross revenue of $5 × 50 = $250. At the $6 price, the theater sells 35 tickets for a gross revenue of $6 × 35 = $210. The difference between these two is $40.*

---

* Gridded-in answers to these problems appear on page 139.

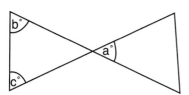

Note: Figure is not drawn to scale

38. In the figure above, what is the value of angle a, if the measure of angle a equals the sum of the measures of angles b and c?

39. How much more is $\frac{1}{2}$ of $\frac{2}{3}$ than $\frac{3}{4}$ of $\frac{1}{3}$?

38.

	/	/	
.	.	.	.
	0	0	0
1	1	1	1
2	2	2	2
3	3	3	3
4	4	4	4
5	5	5	5
6	6	6	6
7	7	7	7
8	8	8	8
9	9	9	9

39.

	/	/	
.	.	.	.
	0	0	0
1	1	1	1
2	2	2	2
3	3	3	3
4	4	4	4
5	5	5	5
6	6	6	6
7	7	7	7
8	8	8	8
9	9	9	9

Answer #38: 90

Theorems: • The sum of the angle measures in a triangle is 180°

• Vertical angles have equal measures

Concept: • Triangle geometry

Vertical angles have the same measure so you know that the angle without a measurement, on the left, is a°—write it in. Now you know all of the angle measures in the triangle on the left, so you can set up the equation $a + b + c = 180$.

You are told in the problem that $a = b + c$, so you can substitute a in for $b + c$ in the equation $a + b + c = 180$ to get $a + a = 180$. Simplifying, you get $a = 90$.

Answer #39: $\dfrac{1}{12}$ or .083

Concept: • Fractions

• $\dfrac{1}{2}$ of $\dfrac{2}{3} = \left(\dfrac{1}{2}\right)\left(\dfrac{2}{3}\right) = \dfrac{1}{3}$

• $\dfrac{3}{4}$ of $\dfrac{1}{3} = \left(\dfrac{3}{4}\right)\left(\dfrac{1}{3}\right) = \dfrac{1}{4}$

• The difference between the two is

• $\dfrac{1}{3} - \dfrac{1}{4} = \dfrac{x4}{3 \times 4} - \dfrac{x3}{4 \times 3}$

$$= \dfrac{4}{12} - \dfrac{3}{12}$$

$$= \dfrac{1}{12}$$

---

* Gridded-in answers to these problems appear on page 139.

40. Adina must read a 100-page book for a class. After an hour she's read 24 pages. Assuming she reads at a constant rate, how long will it take her (in hours) to read the whole book?

41. Find a number between 1 and 100, exclusive, that leaves a remainder of 1 when divided by 6, 14, or 21.

40.

41.

Answer #40: $\dfrac{25}{6}$ or 4.17

Definition: • Rate $= \dfrac{\text{Amount}}{\text{Time}}$

Concept: • Rates

Adina's reading rate is $24 \dfrac{\text{pages}}{\text{hour}}$, and she must read a total of 100 pages. Plugging these values into the equation for rates, you get $24 \dfrac{\text{pages}}{\text{hour}} = \dfrac{100 \text{ pages}}{x \text{ hours}}$. (In this problem, the amount is expressed in pages. In other problems, the amount might be miles or dollars. Problems about rates can deal with anything that occurs over time.)

Canceling out the units in the above equation leaves $24 = \dfrac{100}{x}$. Solving the equation for x yields $\dfrac{100}{24} = \dfrac{25}{6}$. Be careful not to jump too quickly and write $x = .24$; it's an easy error to make, but wrong.

The possible solutions to grid in are either $\dfrac{25}{6}$ or 4.17.*

Answer #41: 43 or 85

Concept: • Factoring and prime factors

The prime factors of 6 are 2 and 3; for 14 they are 2 and 7; and for 21 they are 3 and 7. Therefore, any number that is divisible by 6, 14, and 21 must have 2, 3, and 7 as prime factors. The first such number is the product of 2, 3, and 7: 42. Another such number that is still less than 100 is $42 \times 2 = 84$.

However, you weren't asked to find a number divisible by 6, 14, or 21; you want one that leaves a remainder of 1 when divided by these numbers. If 42 and 84 are divided by these numbers evenly then 43 and 85 must leave a remainder of 1 when divided by 6, 14, and 21.

Now go back and do the division. If you have the time it's a great way to check your work.*

---

* Gridded-in answers to these problems appear on page 140.

42. Find a positive value of a that satisfies the equation $a^2 - 9 = a + 3$.

43. What is the smallest positive number that can be written in the grid?

42.

43.

Answer #42: 4
Theorem: • $a^2 - b^2 = (a - b)(a + b)$
Concept: • Polynomial arithmetic

As with many of the problems, there are many approaches to solving this one. One way is to divide both sides of the equation by $a + 3$. This, however, is dangerous because you run the risk of dividing by zero—how do you know a isn't -3?

A safe approach is to subtract $a + 3$ from both sides of the equation, leaving $a^2 - a - 12$. With a little work you should be able to factor this into $(a - 4)(a + 3) = 0$, and then solve to get $a = 4$ or $a = -3$. The problem specifies that a must be positive so $a = 4.$*

Answer #43: .001
Concept: • Arithmetic

The problem asks for a positive number, so you can't grid in 0. The next larger number is going to be either a fraction or a decimal. You can generate the smallest fraction by making the numerator as small as possible and the denominator as large as possible. With only three digits and a slash to work with—there are only four columns in the grid—you can write the fraction $\frac{1}{99}$.

The smallest decimal you can write is going to start with the decimal point. You want 0 (the fewest) tenths, 0 hundreths, and 1 thousandth, so that the result is not zero. Written out, your solution is .001, or $\frac{1}{1,000}$. $\frac{1}{1,000} < \frac{1}{99}$, the smallest number you can write into the grid is .001.*

---

44. $72.00 is to be divided among Michael, Paul, and Susan in such a way that Michael receives five times as much as Susan, and Paul receives three times as much as Susan. How much does Paul receive? Note: Ignore the dollar sign when gridding in your solution.

45. Consider room temperature to be 74° Fahrenheit. When preheating an oven it takes five seconds for the oven's temperature to rise two degrees. How long, in minutes, should it take to preheat the oven from room temperature to 350° Fahrenheit?

44.

		/	/	
	.	.	.	.
		0	0	0
1	1	1	1
2	2	2	2
3	3	3	3
4	4	4	4
5	5	5	5
6	6	6	6
7	7	7	7
8	8	8	8
9	9	9	9

45.

		/	/	
	.	.	.	.
		0	0	0
1	1	1	1
2	2	2	2
3	3	3	3
4	4	4	4
5	5	5	5
6	6	6	6
7	7	7	7
8	8	8	8
9	9	9	9

Answer #44: 24

Concepts:
- Ratios
- Word problems

Here's one way of solving this problem:

1. Define your variables:
    a. Call the amount Susan receives S
    b. Michael receives $5S$
    c. Paul receives $3S$

2. Set up the equation:

Read:	Write:
a. "72 is . . ."	$72 =$
b. "Among Michael, Paul, and Susan"	$72 = 5S + 3S + S$

3. Solve the equation:
    a. Combine the terms $72 = 9S$
    b. Divide both sides by 9 $8 = S$

4. Since Paul receives three times as much as Susan, Paul receives $3 \times \$8 = \$24$. Don't make the mistake of solving for S and putting down 8 as an answer, because it's not what the question asks.*

Answer #45: 11.5 or $\dfrac{23}{2}$

Definition:
- $\text{Rate} = \dfrac{\text{Amount}}{\text{Time}}$

Concept:
- Rates

The current temperature is $74°$ and the goal is $350°$, so you need to raise the oven's temperature by $350° - 74° = 276°$. You're told it takes five seconds to raise the oven's temperature $2°$, so the heating rate is $\dfrac{2 \text{ degrees}}{5 \text{ degrees}}$.

Now, plug these values into the rate equation to get: $\dfrac{2 \text{ degrees}}{5 \text{ seconds}} = \dfrac{276 \text{ degrees}}{x}$. Canceling two degrees from both sides of the equation you are left with: $\dfrac{1}{5 \text{ seconds}} = \dfrac{138}{x}$. Cross multiplying the two fractions gives you $x = 690$ seconds. The problem asks for the solution in minutes, so you have to divide your solution of 690 seconds by $60 \dfrac{\text{seconds}}{\text{minute}}$. The result is 11.5 (or $\dfrac{23}{2}$) minutes.

---

* Gridded-in answers to these problems appear on page 140.

46. A clothes drawer holds 20 unmatched socks; 10 are identically white and 10 are identically black. If Karen picks out two socks, what is the probability that she will have picked a matching pair, either black or white?

47. Find r if, for all a, p, and q, $a^p = a^{3q}$ and $a^q = a^{4pr}$.

46.

47.

Answer #46: $\dfrac{9}{19}$ or .474

Concept: • Probability

Karen reaches into her drawer and pulls out a sock. That sock will be either white or black. If it's white, there will then be 19 socks (out of the original 20) still in the drawer; 9 of them (out of the original 10) will be white. When Karen reaches into her drawer a second time, there is a 9 in 19, or $\dfrac{9}{19}$, chance that she will pick a second white sock.

The same analysis holds true if the first sock was black. Therefore, the chance of Karen pulling out two socks of the same color is $\dfrac{9}{19}$.

Answer #47: $\dfrac{1}{12}$ or .083

Theorem: • If $a^x = a^y$, then $x = y$

Concept: • Exponents and square roots

Stepping through this problem algebraically is the most straightforward way to solve it:

1. $a^p = a^{3q}$ and $a^q = a^{4pr}$ Given in the problem statement

2. $p = 3q$ and $q = 4pr$ $a^x = a^y$ implies $x = y$

3. $p = 3(4pr)$ Substitute $4pr$ for q in the first equation

4. $p = 12pr$ Simplify

5. $1 = 12r$ Divide both sides of the equation by p

6. $\dfrac{1}{12} = r$ Divide both sides of the equation by 12

48. Grid in a number for which $x^2 < \sqrt{x}$.

49. If $a - b = -11$, $b - c = -13$, and $c - d = 7$, what is the value of $(d - a)$?

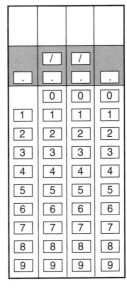

Answer #48:   Any number between 0 and 1, exclusive
Concepts: • Fractions
                 • Exponents and square roots

When you multiply a number by a fraction between 0 and 1, the result is smaller than the original number. For example, $\frac{1}{2}$ of 6 is 3. Consequently, when you square a fraction between 0 and 1 you end up with something smaller than the original fraction.

   The behavior of a square root is just the opposite. When you take the square root of a fraction, you are looking for the fraction that, when multiplied by itself, yields your number. For example, $\sqrt{\frac{9}{25}} = \frac{3}{5}$. So, for any number x between 0 and 1, $\sqrt{x} > x^2$. Note: To grid in the answer for this problem, any number between 0 and 1 will be considered correct; for example, .4.

Answer #49:   17
Concept: • Solving equations

There are two methods to solve multiple equations with multiple unknowns. One is by substitution. The other is to add equations in such a way that variables drop out. This problem lends itself to the latter method.

   Write the equations in such a way that the same variables line up vertically and add the variables downward:

$$
\begin{array}{rrrr}
a - b & & & = -11 \\
 & b - c & & = -13 \\
 & & c - d & = +\,7 \\
\hline
a & & -\,d & = -17
\end{array}
$$

Notice that variables following a negative sign are subtracted instead of added.

   You are asked for the value of $(d - a)$, and you now know that the value of $(a - d)$ is -17. $(d - a)$ is simply $(-1)(a - d) = (-1)(-17) = 17$.

50. A dentist schedules appointments every 15 minutes during the periods:

> 8 a.m. - 10 a.m.
> 10:15 a.m. - 12:15 p.m.
> 12:45 p.m. - 2:45 p.m.
> 3 p.m. - 5 p.m.

If there are no problems during the exam, the appointment requires only 10 minutes; difficult cases require up to 20 minutes. On a particularly difficult day, every appointment took a full 20 minutes. If the dentist worked through her breaks from 10-10:15, 12:15-12:45, and 2:45-3, how long after 5pm, in minutes, did she have to stay at work to see all of her patients?

50.

	/	/	
.	.	.	.
	0	0	0
1	1	1	1
2	2	2	2
3	3	3	3
4	4	4	4
5	5	5	5
6	6	6	6
7	7	7	7
8	8	8	8
9	9	9	9

Answer #50:   100
Concept: • Word problems

The dentist normally works four 2-hour periods for a total of 8 hours. During these 8 hours, she schedules 8 hours ÷ 15 minutes per appointment = 32 appointments. The appointments took 20 minutes each so 32 appointments required 640 minutes or 10 hours and 40 minutes. If the dentist started at 8 a.m. and worked through all of her breaks, she finished by 6:40 p.m., 1 hour and 40 minutes after her normal stopping time of 5 p.m. One hour and 40 minutes is equal to 60 + 40 = 100 minutes.

TEST 2

SECTION 4

This final section of Test 2 consists of ten problems, each of which has five possible answer choices. For each problem, select the answer choice that represents the best solution and shade the corresponding oval.

---

51. Given that $ab \neq 0$ and $a - b \neq 0$, simplify the expression: $\dfrac{1}{\left(\dfrac{1}{a} - \dfrac{1}{b}\right)}$.

   (A) $\dfrac{ab}{a - b}$

   (B) $\dfrac{a - b}{ab}$

   (C) $b - a$

   (D) $\dfrac{ab}{b - a}$

   (E) $\dfrac{b - a}{ab}$

52. The radius of the largest ball that can fit inside a five-inch-tall cylinder with a volume of 20 cubic inches is (in inches):

   (A) 2

   (B) $\dfrac{2}{\sqrt{\pi}}$

   (C) 4

   (D) 4π

   (E) 5

---

51. Ⓐ Ⓑ Ⓒ Ⓓ Ⓔ

52. Ⓐ Ⓑ Ⓒ Ⓓ Ⓔ

127

Answer #51: Ⓓ

Concept: • Fractions

When you see a problem with fractions embedded in fractions, your first thought should be to get rid of them. In this case, you want to multiply the numerator and the denominator of the original fraction by $\dfrac{ab}{ab}$. This doesn't change the value of the fraction because it is just another name for one. However, it does get rid of the $\dfrac{1}{a}$ and $\dfrac{1}{b}$.

$$\frac{1}{\dfrac{1}{a} - \dfrac{1}{b}} \times \frac{ab}{ab} = \frac{ab}{b - a}$$

Answer #52: Ⓑ

Formula: • Volume of a cylinder = $\pi r^2 h$
Concept: • Circle geometry

You are told that the volume of the cylinder is 20 cubic inches and that its height is 5 inches, so you can solve for its radius by setting up the equation 20 = $\pi r^2 5$. Solving for r, you should get $r = \sqrt{\dfrac{4}{\pi}} = \dfrac{2}{\sqrt{\pi}}$.

The radius of the largest ball that can fit inside the cylinder is the smaller of the radius of the cylinder and half of its height, so the answer is B, $\dfrac{2}{\sqrt{\pi}}$.

53. The income tax in a certain state is 5%. Federal income tax regulations allow one to deduct 75% of the amount of one's state income tax. If, as a result, Ann deducts $900 from her federal income tax, what is her income?

(A) $6,000
(B) $7,200
(C) $13,500
(D) $24,000
(E) $33,750

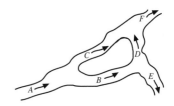

54. The River Paix flows in the directions indicated by the arrows on the above map. If $\frac{5}{8}$ of the water flowing from path A takes path B, and $\frac{3}{5}$ of the water from path B takes path D, then what percentage of the water takes path F?

(A) 25%

(B) $33\frac{1}{3}\%$

(C) $37\frac{1}{2}\%$

(D) $62\frac{1}{2}\%$

(E) 75%

53. Ⓐ Ⓑ Ⓒ Ⓓ Ⓔ

54. Ⓐ Ⓑ Ⓒ Ⓓ Ⓔ

Answer #53: Ⓓ

Concept: • Percentages

Ann deducts $900 from her federal income tax as an allowance for the amount

of state income tax she has paid. As specified, the $900 is 75%, or $\frac{3}{4}$, of the

amount of state income tax paid. To determine this amount, set up the equation

$900 = \frac{3}{4}x$, and solve to get x = $1,200.

The state income tax is 5%, so $1,200 is 5%, or $\frac{1}{20}$, of Ann's income. To

determine Ann's income, set up the equation $1,200 = \frac{1}{20}x$. Solving this yields x

= $24,000.

Answer #54: Ⓔ

Concepts: • Percentages
         • Fractions

You're told that $\frac{5}{8}$ of the water from A flows to B, so put a $\frac{5}{8}$ next to the B branch

of the river. At the same time, you know that the rest of the water goes down

the C branch of the river, so put a $\frac{3}{8}$ next to the C in the diagram.

Then you're told that $\frac{3}{5}$ of the water from the B branch of the river takes

the D branch. Only $\frac{5}{8}$ of the water is flowing down the B branch, so you can't

simply put a $\frac{3}{5}$ on the D branch. Instead, you've got to take what you started

with, the $\frac{5}{8}$ next to B, and multiply it by $\frac{3}{5}$, putting the resulting $\frac{3}{8}$ next to the D

branch.

C and D are the only branches flowing into F, so the amount flowing

through branch F is $\frac{3}{8}$ + $\frac{3}{8}$ = $\frac{6}{8}$ = $\frac{3}{4}$. Another name for $\frac{3}{4}$ is 75%, answer E.

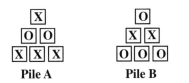

Pile A   **Pile B**

55. How many "X cards" would have to be taken from pile A (leaving the O's where they are) and put in pile B so that the fractional part of X cards is the same for both piles?

(A) None
(B) 1
(C) 2
(D) 3
(E) 4

56. Mark invests $500 each in two stocks, A and B. Stock A costs $100 per share, stock B costs $10 per share. The price per share of each goes up by $1, so Mark sells his stock. What is the difference between the amounts of money Mark earned by investing in the two stocks?

(A) $0
(B) $5
(C) $45
(D) $50
(E) $90

55. (A) (B) (C) (D) (E)

56. (A) (B) (C) (D) (E)

Answer #55: Ⓒ

Concept: • Fractions

There is a way of doing this problem with formulas and equations, but I don't recommend it. Instead, try this approach. Currently, in pile A, $\frac{4}{6}$ of the cards are X's, and in pile B, $\frac{2}{6}$ of the cards are X's. If you move one X card from pile A to pile B, $\frac{3}{5}$ of the cards in pile A and $\frac{3}{7}$ of the cards in pile B would be X's. If you were to take a second X from A and put it in pile B, $\frac{2}{4}$ of the cards in pile A and $\frac{4}{8}$ of the cards in pile B would be X's.

Both $\frac{2}{4}$ and $\frac{4}{8}$ equal $\frac{1}{2}$ so moving two cards from pile A to pile B makes the fractional part of the cards that are X's the same in both piles.

Answer #56: Ⓒ

Concept: • Word problems

With his first $500 Mark was able to buy five shares of stock A at $100 per share. When its value went up by $1 per share and Mark sold it, he earned $5.

With his second $500 Mark was able to buy 50 shares of stock B at $10 per share. When its value went up by $1 per share and Mark sold it, he earned $50.

The difference between what Mark earned by investing in the two stocks is $50 − $5 = $45.

57. In a 365-day year, how many days of the week occur 53 times?

(A) 0
(B) 1
(C) 3
(D) 5
(E) 7

58. Joey's mother is now four times his age. In five years she'll be three times his age. In how many years will she be twice his age?

(A) 5
(B) 10
(C) 15
(D) 20
(E) 25

57. Ⓐ Ⓑ Ⓒ Ⓓ Ⓔ

58. Ⓐ Ⓑ Ⓒ Ⓓ Ⓔ

Answer #57: Ⓑ

Concept: • Repeating sequences☆

The question asks how many times the seven days of the week occur during the year. To figure this out, divide the number of days in the year by the number of days in the week: $365 \div 7 = 52$ with a remainder of 1. The leftover 1 is the one day of the week that will occur a 53rd time during a 365-day year.

Answer #58: Ⓓ

Concept: • Word problems

Call Joey's age j and his mother's age m.

Joey's mother is now four times his age: $m = 4j$

In five years she'll be three times his age: $(m + 5) = 3(j + 5)$

Substituting $4j$ for m in the second equation you get: $(4j + 5) = 3(j + 5)$. Solving for j you get $j = 10$. Plugging $j = 10$ back into either of the two original equations, you can solve for m, which is 40.

Now, when will Joey's mother be twice his age? The equation you need to solve is: $m + x = 2(j + x)$, where x denotes years. Plugging in the values you computed for m and j gives you: $40 + x = 2(10 + x)$. Solving for x, you get $x = 20$.

Now go back and check your answer. Joey is 10 now, and his mother is 40. In five years he'll be 15 and she'll be 45. In twenty years he'll be 30 and she'll be 60. All these numbers fit the problem statement, so you know the answer is correct.

☆ See Concept-to-Problem Index on page 141.

59. A candy company decides to raise the price of its candy bars by 25%. To "hide" the increase from consumers, the company also increases the size of the candy bar by 20%. By what percentage was the price per size increased?

(A) $1\frac{1}{4}\%$

(B) $4\frac{1}{6}\%$

(C) 5%

(D) 20%

(E) 25%

60. Emily buys 100 ft. of fencing in order to build a garden. What is the ratio of the area she can enclose in a circular garden to the area she can enclose in a square garden?

(A) $4 : \pi$
(B) $\pi : 4$
(C) $4 : \pi^2$
(D) $16 : \pi^2$
(E) $\pi^2 : 16$

59. Ⓐ Ⓑ Ⓒ Ⓓ Ⓔ

60. Ⓐ Ⓑ Ⓒ Ⓓ Ⓔ

Answer #59: Ⓑ

Concepts: • Percentages
                  • Calculator usuage☆

ETS recently changed its rules to allow the use of calculators on the SAT. However, very few problems make use of them, and those that do only do so minimally. This problem can make use of a calculator toward the end.

To solve this problem, let P = original price and S = original size; thus, $\dfrac{P}{S}$ represents the oringal price per size. The new price is 25% more, or 1.25P, and the new size is 20% more, or 1.2S. So, the new price per size is $\dfrac{1.25P}{1.2S}$. To find the percent change, use your calculator to compute that the decimal form of $\dfrac{1.25}{1.2}$ is 1.041666. . . . Therefore, the new price per size is .0416 . . . more than the old or 4.166 . . .% Note that .16666. . . . written in a fractional form is $\dfrac{1}{6}$ so the correct solution is $4\dfrac{1}{6}$%, answer B.

Answer #60: Ⓐ

Formulas: • Area of a circle = πr^2
                  • Circumference of a circle = 2D = $2\pi r$
                  • Area of a square = s^2
                  • Perimeter of a square = $4s$

Concepts: • Circle geometry
                  • Rectangle geometry

A circular fence with a circumference of 100 has a radius of $\dfrac{100}{2\pi} = \dfrac{50}{\pi}$. The area of this circle is $\pi\left(\dfrac{50}{\pi}\right)^2 = \dfrac{50^2}{\pi}$.

A square fence with a perimeter of 100 has a side of length $\dfrac{100}{4} = 25$. The area of this square is 25^2.

The ratio of the area of the circle to the area of the square is therefore $\dfrac{50^2}{\pi} : 25^2$, which is the same as $\dfrac{25^2 \times 2^2}{\pi} : 25^2$. Dividing both sides of the ratio by 25^2 and multiplying both sides by π leaves a ratio of 4 : π, answer A.

SOLUTIONS TO GRID-IN PROBLEMS FOR TEST 1

41.

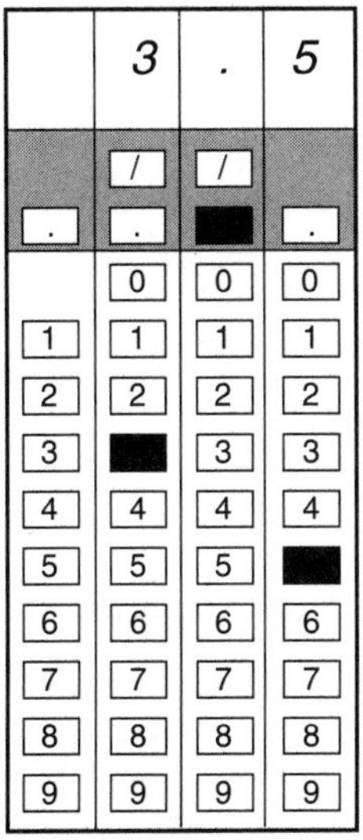

```
    3  .  5
```
Answer gridded: 3.5

42.

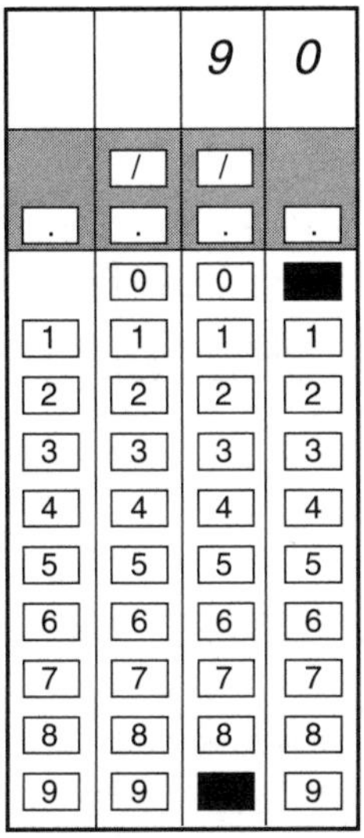

```
       9  0
```
Answer gridded: 90

43.

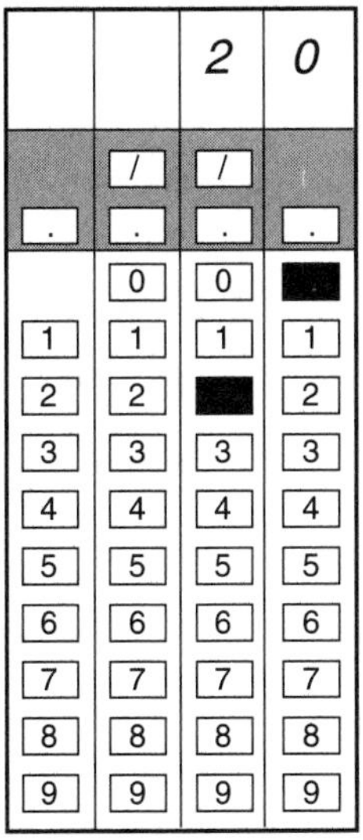

```
       2  0
```
Answer gridded: 20

44.

```
          5
```
Answer gridded: 5

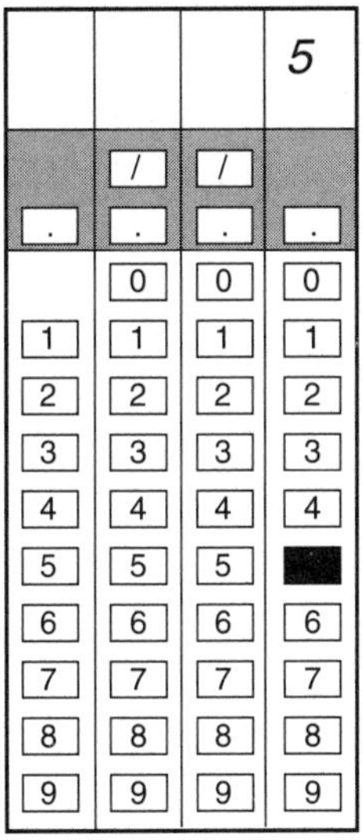

45. `3`

46. `2 6 1`

47. `4 / 3`

48. `6`

49. `3 6`

50. `. 6 6 7`

36.

			1
	/	/	
.	.	.	.
	0	0	0
1	1	1	■
2	2	2	2
3	3	3	3
4	4	4	4
5	5	5	5
6	6	6	6
7	7	7	7
8	8	8	8
9	9	9	9

37.

		4	0
	/	/	
.	.	.	.
	0	0	■
1	1	1	1
2	2	2	2
3	3	3	3
4	4	■	4
5	5	5	5
6	6	6	6
7	7	7	7
8	8	8	8
9	9	9	9

38.

		9	0
	/	/	
.	.	.	.
	0	0	■
1	1	1	1
2	2	2	2
3	3	3	3
4	4	4	4
5	5	5	5
6	6	6	6
7	7	7	7
8	8	8	8
9	9	■	9

39.

1	/	1	2
	■	/	
.	.	.	.
	0	0	0
■	1	■	1
2	2	2	■
3	3	3	3
4	4	4	4
5	5	5	5
6	6	6	6
7	7	7	7
8	8	8	8
9	9	9	9

40. 4 . 1 7

41. 8 5

42. 4

43. . 0 0 1

44. 2 4

45. 2 3 / 2

CONCEPT-TO-PROBLEM INDEX

Each problem on the SAT tests one or more math concepts. This index lists the 120 problems in this book by the concepts each tests. As you are working the two SAT tests, circle in this index the problem numbers that you get wrong or have difficulty with. When you are done with the tests, you can then look at this index and clearly identify those skills that you need to practice. Conversely, you can use this index to get directly to those types of problems you now you need help with. Those concepts in the tests that come under the "other" category are written with a star (☆) following them. For example, problem 6 on page 9 tests the concept of repeating sequences. (Note: The numbers listed for each concept refer to the test number, problem number, and page number. For example, 1-25(29) refers to test 1, problem 25, which appears on page 29.)

Algebra

Averages. . . . . 1-22(25), 1-36(43), 1-49(59), 1-57(67), 2-5(75), 2-21(93), 2-29(101), 2-31(103)

Functions . . . . 1-15(19), 1-34(41), 2-20(89), 2-21(93)

Probability . . . . 1-21(25), 1-55(65), 2-46(121)

Rates . . . . 1-5(9), 1-10(13), 1-12(15), 1-16(19), 1-17(21), 1-42(51), 1-60(69), 2-14(83), 2-40(115), 2-45(119)

Solving equations . . . . 1-41(51), 2-9(79), 2-16(85), 2-49(123)

Word problems . . . . 1-3(7), 1-9(13), 1-15(19), 1-24(27), 2-15(85), 2-37(111), 2-44(119), 2-50(125), 2-56(131), 2-58(133)

Arithmetic

Arithmetic . . . . 1-7(11), 1-8(11), 1-15(19), 1-25(29), 1-28(35), 1-31(37), 1-44(53), 1-51(61), 2-1(71), 2-6(75), 2-18(87), 2-25(97), 2-26(97), 2-43(117)